INTERMEDIATE HISTORY

FROM THE CRADLE TO THE GRAVE
SOCIAL WELFARE IN BRITAIN 1890s – 1950

SIMON WOOD
& CLAIRE WOOD

Hodder Gibson

A MEMBER OF THE HODDER HEADLINE GROUP

Acknowledgements

The publishers would like to thank the following individuals, institutions and companies for permission to reproduce photographs in this book. Every effort has been made to trace ownership of copyright. The publishers would be happy to make arrangements with any copyright holder whom it has not been possible to contact.

Bridgeman Art Library 18; Daily Mirror 77 (left); David Low, Evening Standard/Centre for Study of Cartoons and Caricatures, University of Kent at Canterbury 62 (right), 74 (bottom), 77 (right), 79, 86; Heatherbank Museum of Social Work 9, 17, 50 (top); Hulton Archive 11, 23, 31, 39 (top), 49, 56, 58, 62, 67 (top right and bottom), 74 (top), 78, 83, 87 (both), 90, 92 (both); John Frost Newspapers 71; Mary Evans Picture Library 35, 50 (bottom), 91; Outram Picture Archive 66; National Museum of Scotland, Scottish Life Archive 4 (bottom), 10, 14, 61; People's History Museum Textile Conservation Studio and Labour History Archive and Study Centre 28; Punch 32, 39 (bottom), 40, 42, 46, 53, 70, 89; The Annan Gallery 4 (top); Topham Picturepoint 67 (top left);

Orders: please contact Bookpoint Ltd, 130 Milton Park, Abingdon, Oxon OX14 4SB. Telephone: (44) 01235 827720, Fax: (44) 01235 400454. Lines are open from 9.00–5.00, Monday to Saturday, with a 24 hour message answering service. You can also order through our website www.hoddereducation.co.uk

British Library Cataloguing in Publication Data

A catalogue record for this title is available from The British Library

ISBN-13: 978-0-340-84629-2

Published by Hodder Gibson, 2a Christie Street, Paisley PA1 1NB.
Tel: 0141 848 1609; Fax: 0141 889 6315; email: hoddergibson@hodder.co.uk

First published 2002
Impression number   10 9 8 7 6
Year   2008

Copyright © 2002 Simon Wood and Claire Wood

Hachette's policy is to use papers that are natural, renewable and recyclable products and made from wood grown in sustainable forests. The logging and manufacturing processes are expected to conform to the environmental regulations of the country of origin.

Cover photo Applicants for Admission to a Casual Ward, 1874 by Sir Luke Fildes, Royal Holloway, University of London/Bridgeman Art Library
Illustrated by Chartwell Illustrators and Ian Heard
Typeset by Fakenham Photosetting Ltd, Fakenham, Norfolk
Printed in Great Britain for Hodder Gibson, 2a Christie Street, Paisley, PA1 1NB, Scotland, UK by Martins The Printers, Berwick-Upon-Tweed.

CONTENTS

INTRODUCTION

Look at the picture.

- ◆ How can you tell this child is poor?
- ◆ Can you guess why this child is poor?
- ◆ Do you think that the government ought to help this child?
- ◆ What sort of help should be given to this child?

Today we would take it for granted that social services would be involved in trying to help this child escape from poverty. We would react with shock and disgust if social workers failed to protect this poor and vulnerable child.

It is not only in times of crisis that we expect help from the Government. Today we are provided with help to make sure we are looked after at difficult times in our lives.

- ◆ We are born in a National Health Service hospital.
- ◆ We can choose to go to a state-funded school.
- ◆ When we are ill we go to the state-funded doctor.
- ◆ If we lose our job we get state help to find another job and money to live on when unemployed.
- ◆ When we are old we get a state pension.

'From the cradle to the grave', we expect the Government to assist us with our needs. However, at the end of the 19th century people thought differently. They thought that if you were poor it was your own fault: the cause of your poverty was some physical or mental flaw. There was little state help. British society did not take collective responsibility for the welfare of its citizens.

Poverty means a person is unable to afford the basic needs of life. These could include food, housing, heating and clothing. People who don't have these things are described as living below the 'poverty line'. However, being poor can mean different things to different people depending on the time being studied and the country being looked at. What it meant to be poor changed greatly in Britain between 1890 and 1951.

This book is about how and why attitudes to poverty changed, and how and why Britain built up its 'welfare' system in the 20th century. By 1951, most of the social services that we call the 'welfare state' had been set up. It was a great achievement, but arguments continue about how much help a government should give its people and who pays for this help.

BRITAIN AT THE END OF THE 19TH CENTURY

In this chapter you will find out about:
- Why Britain was a rich and powerful country
- How Britain was ruled
- What people thought about Britain at the time
- What people in Britain were worried about

QUESTION

Why do you think having a large Empire helped to make Britain powerful?

WHAT WAS BRITAIN LIKE BY 1900?

By 1900 Britain was one of the world's richest and strongest countries. Britain was an Empire, controlling land across the continents of the globe. A powerful navy controlled the seas across which British ships traded.

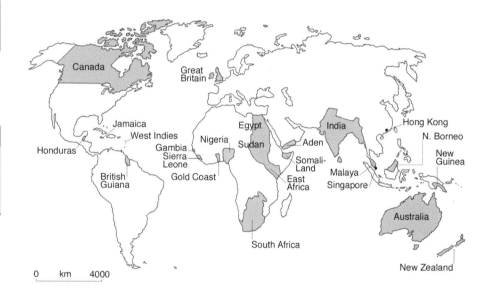

SOURCE 1.1

Map of the world showing the extent of the British Empire.

FACTFILE

The Industrial Revolution

The Industrial Revolution is a term used to describe the process of producing goods in factories using machinery, rather than at home using hand power. A Scottish inventor, James Watt, improved early steam engine design, making them more efficient. Steam engines powered the factories where more machinery speeded up the production of cotton, wool and other goods. Britain had good supplies of coal, to power the engines, and iron, which was used in the production of ships and railways. She also had a skilled workforce and a good banking system, which financed this change in working. During the 19th century Britain dominated the world in terms of her economic power. Power, which was created by this Industrial Revolution.

One reason that Britain was so wealthy and powerful was due to the fact that she had been the first country to industrialise.

The Industrial Revolution had brought wealth and importance to Britain. However, most of this wealth was in the hands of a small number of people. There was a growing middle class of merchants, bankers, ironmasters and factory bosses, but most of the population were working class. Even within this large group there were differences. Skilled workers such as engineers and craftsmen lived well, but manual labourers did not. The following sources show the conditions that many people lived in.

SOURCE 1.2

A corner of George Street and High Street in Glasgow. Taken at the end of the 19th century, it shows the poor housing that many people lived in. Overcrowding was common and the housing caused diseases to spread easily.

SOURCE 1.3

c. 1900, 'The Lee' Edinburgh

HOW WAS BRITAIN GOVERNED?

Britain was a constitutional monarchy. Under Queen Victoria (1837–1901) Britain's power had grown. When she died, Victoria's rule was followed by her son, King Edward VII (1901–1910). British monarchs had little power. Real power to make laws, lay with the two Houses of Parliament; the House of Commons and the House of Lords. British politics was dominated by the Conservative and Liberal parties during the 19th century. This changed as more men were given the vote in General Elections. The Labour Representation Committee (the Labour Party from 1906) emerged in 1900, as a result of more working men being given the vote. By 1900 two out of three men had the vote.

THE ROLE OF GOVERNMENT

Unlike today the Government had a very small role in everyday life. By 1890 the role of the government within Britain was:
◆ to provide control of the workplace
◆ to provide minimum standards of public health
◆ to provide limited education
◆ to provide limited help for the poor in society who deserved to be helped.

WHAT DID BRITISH PEOPLE THINK ABOUT THEIR COUNTRY?

The British were very proud of their Empire. The song, 'Land of Hope and Glory' shows what many people felt.

SOURCE 1.4

'Land of Hope and Glory, Mother of the Free,
How shall we extol thee, who are born of thee?
Wider still and wider shall thy bounds be set;
God who made thee mighty, make thee mightier yet.'

WORRIES: ECONOMIC DECLINE?

There were times when unemployment increased due to trade depressions. An important economic depression happened in the 1870s and 1880s due to increased competition from the United States of America and Germany. These countries industrialised later than Britain, but took advantage of the fact that they had up-to-date technology and vast natural resources. Britain, by the 1890s, had not kept up with technological developments and new industries like the production of chemicals. This threat to her economic power worried people at the time. They wondered what had caused it and what could be done to make sure that Britain remained powerful.

SOURCE 1.5

Table 1 Population (millions)

Year (approx.)	USA	Britain	Germany
1870	39.9	26.1	41.1
1900	76.1	37.0	56.4
1910	92.4	40.8	64.9

Table 2 Share of World Industrial Production

Year (approx.)	USA	Britain	Germany
1870	23	32	13
1896–1900	30	20	17
1913	36	14	16

Table 3 Share of World Trade

Year (approx.)	USA	Britain	Germany
1870	8	25	10
1901–05	11	16	12
1913	11	16	12

WORRIES: POVERTY?

There was also growing concern about the poorer classes in society. By 1900 a number of books had been published that described in great detail, how the poor lived. These books were widely read by the more educated members of society. What they read horrified them. How much poverty existed in Britain and what did this mean for the country? Was this poverty a reason why Britain was falling behind her industrial rivals? What should the Government do about poverty? In 1883 Andrew Mearns published a book called *The Bitter Cry of Outcast London, An Enquiry into the Condition of the Abject Poor*. Below he describes dreadful poverty that led to appalling living conditions.

SOURCE 1.6

Every room in these rotten and reeking tenements houses a family, often two. In one cellar a sanitary inspector reports finding a father, mother, three children, and four pigs! In another room a missionary found a man ill with small-pox, his wife just recovering from her eighth confinement [birth], and the children running about half naked and covered with dirt. Here are seven people living in one underground kitchen and a little dead child lying in the same room. Elsewhere is a poor widow, her three children, and a child who has been dead thirteen days.

Writers such as William Booth, the founder of the Salvation Army, had also begun to write about poverty. William Booth's book, *In Darkest England and the Way Out* (1890) described living conditions unknown to wealthy people. Britain was the richest country in the world but many people lived in dirty, overcrowded housing, begged for money and lived dreadful lives.

SOURCE 1.7

Paul de Rousiers a French visitor to London described the East End of London in a book called *The Labour Question in Britain*. He described:
A population in abject poverty, squalid, wan, and forbidding in appearance, seethes in the narrow, dirty, muddy, reeking streets.

The educated and wealthier people who lived in Britain in 1890 may have been interested in poverty. What they did not yet know was how much poverty existed in their country. In fact they had some strange ideas as to what caused poverty and what help the state should provide.

Chapter summary
- Britain was a rich and powerful country by 1890.
- This was due to the Industrial Revolution and her Empire.
- Within Britain there was great wealth and great poverty.
- By 1890 there was worry about the declining power of Britain and the increase in poverty.

QUESTION PRACTICE

Intermediate 1

1 Look at Sources 1.2 and 1.6. Describe the housing many people lived in by 1900. *Outcome 1*

SOURCE A

Table 3 *Share of World Trade*

Year (approx.)	USA	Britain	Germany
1870	8	25	10
1901–05	11	16	12
1913	11	16	12

2 Look at Table 3. Why were people worried about Britain's place as the leading world power by 1900? *Outcome 2*

Intermediate 2

1 Source B is from *In Darkest England and the Way Out* by William Booth.

Darkest England, like Darkest Africa, reeks with malaria. The foul and fetid breath of our slums is almost as poisonous as that of the African swamp.

Explain why people in Britain were becoming increasingly concerned about poverty by 1900. *Outcome 2*

2 THE POOR LAW SYSTEM

By 1890 there was not much 'help' provided by the Government for those who were very poor. The existence of very poor people was a worry to the rulers of Britain. They felt that such people should not really exist in a wealthy country. The system of help provided was based on the 1834 Poor Law Amendment Act in England and Wales and the 1845 Poor Law Amendment Act in Scotland. Help for the poor was called *relief* in the language of the time. Outdoor relief refers to help (money or goods) given to the poor in their own home. Indoor relief refers to help given in the workhouse or poorhouse.

SOURCE 2.1

The Poor Law Amendment Act of 1834, (England and Wales)
♦ Geographical areas called parishes (an area around a church) were to be grouped into 'Unions' with a central *workhouse*.
♦ Those in need of help because they were very poor had to prove they were poor. If they could prove they were poor they were allowed into the workhouse.
♦ Inside the workhouse, life was made so unattractive that it was less 'eligible' (less likely to be chosen) than the lowest paid employment outside the workhouse.
♦ No help for the able-bodied poor was to be made available outside the workhouse. If you were able-bodied (fit) you should be able to find work.

1845 Poor Law Amendment Act (Scotland). In Scotland the situation was different.
♦ Poorhouses were built and local Boards were elected to run them.
♦ The able-bodied poor, without work, had no right to help.
♦ Only the disabled, widows and deserted wives with children, orphans under 12 (girls) or 14 (boys) and the old and sick had a right to help from the poorhouse.
♦ Poorhouses were not as harsh as the workhouse in England. For example, inmates were not forced to work.

SOURCE 2.2

View of Barnhill Poorhouse in Springburn, Glasgow. In the 1900s it housed 2,000 inmates and had 61 staff.

WAS THIS SYSTEM SUCCESSFUL IN DEALING WITH POVERTY?

1 The short answer to this question is 'no'. The Poor Law was designed to deal with poverty in the countryside. Britain was an industrial country with people working in factories. More and more people were living in towns as a result. The Poor Law could not hope to deal with the massive amounts of unemployment that were created when factories went out of business. The system could not cope with the scale of poverty in Britain.

2 The workhouse system was hated by the poor. To go to a workhouse was a humiliating experience and, as intended, was the last resort of the poor. There was fierce opposition in Wales and the North of England in particular. They were like prisons to many people. The conditions inside the workhouses were often exaggerated but some general points can be made.

   ◆ The work provided for the inmates of the workhouse was boring and very repetitive.
   ◆ Families were separated in the workhouse. Children, adult males and females could not live together within the workhouse walls.

SOURCE 2.3

Charles Chaplin remembered going to the workhouse as a boy. He was born in 1889 in London.

There was no alternative: she (Chaplin's mother) was burdened with two children, and in poor health; and so she decided that the three of us should enter the Lambeth workhouse ... there we were made to separate. Mother going in one direction to the women's ward and we in another to the children's. How well I remember the sadness of that first visiting day: the shock of seeing Mother enter the visiting-room garbed in workhouse clothes. How forlorn and embarrassed she looked.

SOURCE 2.4

A women's ward

♦ Food was monotonous and based on cheap products. Meat was only given twice a week. There were exceptions to this, for example, in 1845 at a workhouse in Andover, starving paupers were discovered eating the marrow from the bones that had been supplied to the workhouse for crushing.

Richard Oastler, writing in 1841, studied the food on offer to an inmate of the poorhouse and concluded that the diet was worse than that available to prisoners in jail. He concluded that:

SOURCE 2.5

... under the accursed new Poor Law, poverty is in England punished with greater severity than crime! ... I can do more. My heart bleeds – my head is bewildered. The sins of England make me tremble for my native land! Under the operation of the new Poor Law, England is reduced to a state of horrid barbarism.

♦ Discipline within the workhouse was strict.

What the Poor Law system did that was successful was to make state help unattractive to many poor people. It has been calculated that 90% of the unemployed never touched poor relief even though they lived in poverty.

WHY WAS THIS SYSTEM SO HARSH?

Behind such a system was a set of beliefs about what made people poor and therefore how they should be treated. Those that ran the country felt that:

If too much help was provided by the Government for the poor, this would encourage the poor not to look for work. Living on Government help would be seen as being easier than getting a job. This was expensive as more poor people would rely on state help rather than their own efforts to escape poverty.

The amount of help given to the poor was at a very low level and stopped people from seeking that help. Those that were poor had to look after themselves. Saving money, living a sober life and working hard to help yourself was the best way to avoid poverty. If you had to come to the workhouse you had obviously failed to do this. This was seen as a sign of a failing in character. You must be either idle, spending too much money, or a drunk if you could not look after yourself.

To be poor was to belong to a class of people who were considered to be very different from the rest of society. The views in the quote below were common in Britain.

SOURCE 2.7

The inmates of a workhouse in London, England at the beginning of the 20th century. Such 'paupers' were not considered to be proper human beings by many people.

SOURCE 2.6

From Helen Bosanquet, *The Strength of the People*, 1902.
To have classified a man as belonging to the poor ... means that we no longer expect from him the qualities of independence and responsibility which we assume as a matter of course in all others. ... we cannot expect him to be a good workman even in his own degree; he is one of the submerged, then we deny him all manliness, and expect no effort on his part to raise himself above the waves; he lives in a slum or a ghetto or a mean street, it is impossible, then, for him to have any intelligent interests or amusements, or be anything but a drinking brute.

Chapter summary
- The Government provided limited help to those who were very poor.
- This help was found in the workhouse in England and the poorhouse in Scotland.
- Conditions in the workhouse were deliberately harsh to stop people seeking help.
- Those that sought help were thought to suffer from some personal failing.
- In reality the Poor Law could not cope with the scale of poverty.

QUESTION PRACTICE

Intermediate 1

Source A is by a man called J.F. Oakeshott in 1894. Oakeshott was a Socialist who did not like the workhouse system.

... many men and women every year deliberately prefer death by starvation outside the workhouse to accepting relief from the rates [the workhouse] with its deprivation of the privileges of citizenship and its dishonourable stigma of pauperism on aged and young, infirm and able-bodied, deserving and undeserving alike ...

1 Study Source A and use your own knowledge to explain why many people disliked going to the poorhouse. *Outcome 2*

2 Look at Source 2.3.
How valuable is Source 2.3 for a study of conditions in a poorhouse? *Outcome 3*

Intermediate 2

1 Explain why the poor law system was so harsh. *Outcome 2*

3 SELF-HELP

In the last chapter the idea of self-help was mentioned. This was very important, as many people believed this was the best way to avoid poverty. One of the most important people who believed in this was Samuel Smiles (1812–1904), a Scot.

Samuel Smiles was born in Haddington, East Lothian in 1812. He qualified as a doctor from Edinburgh University. Today he is remembered for his writings. His most famous and important book was called *Self-Help* and was published in 1859. This idea of self-help was very popular in the 19th and early 20th centuries.

Smiles believed that effort and positive thinking could make anything possible. Such ideas were important because they helped create a spirit of industry and enterprise that encouraged people to improve themselves, through hard work. Ideas led to inventions, which led to the making of fortunes. It was the ideas and inventions that had made Britain rich through the Industrial Revolution. Smiles argued that:

SOURCE 3.1

'Heaven helps those who help themselves' is a well tried maxim, embodying in a small compass the results of vast human experience. The spirit of self-help is the root of all genuine growth in the individual; and, exhibited in the lives of the many, it constitutes the true source of national strength and vigour.

Smiles warned against governments helping people too much. This help was bad because it made men helpless. The role of governments should be very limited.

SOURCE 3.2

Whatever is done for man or classes, to a certain extent takes away the stimulus and necessity of doing for themselves; and where men are subjected to over-guidance and over government, the inevitable tendency is to render them comparatively helpless. ... it is every day becoming more clearly understood, that the function of government is negative and restrictive, rather than positive and active.

This belief in self-help is important because it led many people in Britain to believe that poverty could be beaten, by positive thinking and hard work alone. Smiles himself said that any help given by the Government to the poor was useless because:

SOURCE 3.3

No laws, however stringent, can make the idle industrious, the thriftless provident, or the drunken sober.

The only way for the individual to escape poverty was through their own efforts:

SOURCE 3.4

Only be effected by means of individual action, economy, and self-denial; by better habits, rather than by greater rights.

The average worker could avoid poverty by working hard and saving some of their wages. These savings could be used whenever the worker was out of a job, or became unable to work because of illness or old age.

There was no need for the Government to become involved in providing for the poor under such a way of thinking. It was the duty of the individual to look after themselves. Those that did not were either idle, unable or unwilling to save, or drunks.

WHAT SELF-HELP WAS THERE?

Self-help worked for those members of the working class who had a regular income, large enough to allow savings to be made. These workers tended to be skilled. There were many places where they could save money to provide for illness, unemployment and old age.

FRIENDLY SOCIETIES

Friendly Societies were the most popular way in which people helped themselves. Benefits were given out based on the contributions an individual made. J. Tidd Pratt, in his book, *Suggestions for the Establishment of Friendly Societies* (1855), summed up the ideas behind Friendly Societies very well.

SOURCE 3.5

Friendly Societies are formed on the principle of mutual insurance. Each member contributes a certain sum by weekly or monthly subscriptions while he is in health, for which he expects to receive from the society a certain provision or allowance when he is incapacitated for work by accident, sickness, or old age.

By the 1890s it was estimated that 8,000,000 people had made some sort of contribution to a Friendly Society. Most friendly societies also ran social activities, such as an annual parade or gala day.

SAVINGS BANKS

These were very popular with servants and those who were saving for their children. There were even 'penny savings banks', which were aimed at the very poor, who could only save very small amounts of money. The increasing numbers who used these banks during the 19th century was a good sign according to some. Savings meant people had money at times of difficulty. It also encouraged good habits and behaviour.

SOURCE 3.6

From William Lewis, *A History of the Banks for Saving*, 1866.
... we see more in Savings Banks than that they enabled many in times of hardship by a wise foresight to escape much that others suffered. Savings Banks created and then fostered habits of economy and frugality, and every man won over to the pursuit and practice of these habits increased the sum of prosperity ... during the period we are considering.

The Post Office also opened Savings Accounts. These were extremely popular, with 663,000 opening accounts in 1863–68. They grew to 5,776,000 by the 1890s.

THE CO-OPERATIVE MOVEMENT

SOURCE 3.7

The Falkland Equitable Co-operative Society c. 1890.

Members of the working class had helped themselves by forming Co-operative Societies. This involved a community getting together to provide low cost food and services for themselves. For example, a grocery store or a funeral parlour.

Not everyone liked the idea of self-help. The people who were critical of self-help pointed out that not all people could save for a 'rainy day'. Henry Mayhew in his great study of *London Labour and the London Poor (1861)* identified that casual labourers were unable to save regularly because they did not have regular employment. Such people did not think about saving money so Mayhew concluded that:

SOURCE 3.8

The ordinary effects of uncertain labour, then, are to drive the labourers to improvidence, recklessness, and pauperism.

Lack of education and poor health also stopped many people improving their lives. It was not possible for everybody to improve their life by positive thinking alone.

Chapter summary
- Self-help meant that people could escape poverty by saving money and living a sensible life. Such ideas were very popular.
- The working class were encouraged to save through organisations like Friendly Societies and Savings Banks.
- The working class helped themselves by setting up co-operative stores to provide good food at a fair price.
- Not everybody believed that all poor people could save money for a 'rainy day'.

QUESTION PRACTICE

Intermediate 1

1 Study Source 3.4
   Use this source and your own knowledge to explain what Samuel Smiles believed about how people could escape from poverty. *Outcome 2*

Intermediate 2

1 Describe the ways in which the working class were encouraged to help themselves. *Outcome 1*

2 How useful is Source 3.1 for somebody studying this topic? *Outcome 3*

4 VOLUNTARY AID: CHARITY

In this chapter you will find out about:
◆ Why charity was important in helping the poor
◆ Why people were involved in running charities
◆ The attitudes of people running charities towards the poor

QUESTION

Do you think that help for the poor should be provided by the Government or charities?

The Poor Law was help provided by the Government for the very poor. Further help came from the many charities that were founded during the 19th century. Charities provided a range of help:
◆ giving money to the poor
◆ giving time to help the poor
◆ providing some particular expertise to help the poor.

Many of these charities, such as the *RSPCA*, *Dr. Barnado's* and the *Salvation Army* continue to exist today. There were a huge number of charities. One survey of London in 1861 identified no fewer than 640 charitable organisations helping the poor. This help ranged from hospitals for the ill and orphanages, to Bible missionary activities.

Charity was so important that one historian has commented:

SOURCE 4.1

Private charity in the eighteenth and nineteenth centuries was far more important than the poor law in the day-to-day relief of poverty.

In Scotland the need for charity was even greater as the official Poor Law gave help to a very small group of the poor. The only groups to get help would be the old, the young and the disabled. Scottish charities were very important in helping the poor. The 1897 report of the Annual Conference of the Charity Organisation Society calculated that Glasgow Charities raised £1,000,000 per year while the Edinburgh Charities raised £250,000 per year.

Most charities providing help for the poor were frequently organised by well-meaning middle-class men and women. These people had a number of reasons for running charities.
◆ Fear that the poor would rise up against those wealthier than themselves in revolution. Charity would stop this.
◆ Genuine concern. Many charities were motivated by Christian concern for the plight of their fellow man and woman.
◆ It was an opportunity for middle-class women to get involved in public life. By 1900 professions were opening up to women but charities remained an area where women could organise and make a real difference.
◆ The desire to help the poor lead a 'better' life.

Those running charities did not see poverty as the result of an economic system that made people unemployed. Most believed that poverty was caused by the people who were poor themselves. They had some personal failing that made them poor. Most people who ran charities were strong believers in the ideas of Samuel Smiles.

A typical example of the well-meaning individual who provided charity was that of Octavia Hill (1838–1912). Octavia Hill was a middle-class lady. She was interested in the link between poverty and bad housing. She believed that slums were created because of landlords who did not care about maintaining their properties. The tenants in these properties also helped create these slums by their bad behaviour and happiness to live in squalor. Hill sought to change this by managing property in a better way. She made sure that the properties she managed were well maintained. In return, she expected her tenants to pay their rent on time and to live respectable and responsible lives. Charity to Octavia Hill meant the education of the poor in how to lead better lives. This was the responsibility of people like herself. She was totally against state help for the poor.

Hill believed that charity that was given to the poor, without any idea of how it was spent, was a bad thing because:

SOURCE 4.3

You discourage the habit of belonging to clubs, the habit of saving, the habit of purchasing things, and possessing things; you bring side by side the man who has laid by nothing, and who is well cared for at a time when misfortune comes to him, and the man who has sacrificed something through his time of steady work, and on whom the whole burden falls when misfortune comes, he having to spend his savings, whereas the other man is helped from outside [by charity].

Hill's beliefs were very common among those who provided charity. In providing charity you were also responsible for improving the way the poor led their lives.

SOURCE 4.4

From Samuel Barnett, 'Charity up to date', in The Contemporary Review, 1912. Charities should aim at encouraging growth rather than at giving relief. They should be inspired by hope rather than pity. They should be a means of education, a means of enabling the recipient to increase in bodily, mental, or spiritual strength. If I spend twenty shillings on giving a dinner or a night's lodging to twenty vagrants, I have done nothing to make them stronger workers or better citizens. I have only kept poverty alive; but if I spend the same sum in sending one person to a convalescent hospital, he will be at any rate a stronger man, and if during his stay at the hospital his mind is interested in some subject – in something not himself – he will probably be a happier man.

Such people as Hill and Barnett tended to be members of the Charity Organisation Society (C.O.S.), which was founded in 1869. The Charity Organisation Society felt that the type of help given should relate to the particular circumstances of the person seeking help. Charity must do more than simply give help. The help must have a purpose.

SOURCE 4.2

Octavia Hill.

SOURCE 4.6

A Salvation Army poster advertises William Booth's farm colonies in Essex and Hertfordshire. These colonies were where those who had been saved from the misery of the cities would find a new life.

SOURCE 4.5

The Charity Organisation Society aims at helping cases, if possible, in such a way as to make the benefit permanent. It always endeavours, if it can, to give a man such help as will enable him to be afterwards independent of charity altogether.

There were other reasons for starting charities. Many were religious in origin. One of the most famous individuals was William Booth (1829–1919).

In 1861 he started the *Salvation Army*. To begin with he hoped to save souls by converting the poor to God. He came to believe that his religious campaign would never be successful unless poverty was ended. He hoped to achieve this by setting up work colonies where the poor could be re-trained and live more productive lives (see source 14.6).

Again, Booth hoped to improve the lot of the poor through re-training. Improve the individual and you would end poverty. As Booth said:

SOURCE 4.7

To get a man soundly saved it is not enough to put on him a pair of new breeches, to give him regular work, or even to give him a University education. These things are all outside a man, and if the inside remains unchanged you have wasted your labour.

In reality this link was not a clear one. The existence of so many charities was evidence that not everybody who was poor could improve themselves and escape poverty. Few people would admit to this in the 1890s. However, the attitudes behind charity were soon to be challenged by studies that would show that poverty had complicated and varied causes. It was by no means clear that the only cause of poverty was the person who was poor.

Chapter summary
- Charities were very important in helping those who were poor.
- Charitable help was given for a number of reasons.
- Charity sought to help people by improving the way in which they led their lives.

QUESTION PRACTICE

Intermediate 1

SOURCE A

... It is more important to raise self-respect and develop taste than just to meet physical needs.

1 Use Source A and your own knowledge to explain why many charities sought to change the way the poor led their lives.

Outcome 2

Intermediate 2

1 Describe the reasons why so many middle and upper-class people became involved in providing charity for the poor.

Outcome 1

5

WHY DID ATTITUDES TOWARDS POVERTY CHANGE? THE SURVEYS OF BOOTH AND ROWNTREE

In this chapter you will find out:
- Who Charles Booth was
- Who Seebohm Rowntree was
- What they found out about poverty in the surveys they carried out
- Why these surveys were so important

Two men became well known as a result of the work they did studying poverty in Britain. Charles Booth and Seebohm Rowntree were both wealthy men who studied the poor.

The books of people like Andrew Mearns (see Chapter 1) shocked the wealthy Victorians. Charles Booth was one such man. He was originally a Liverpool ship-owner. At first he believed that the level of poverty in Britain was limited and could be dealt with by charity. In common with most people of his class, he originally believed that if people were poor it was their own fault.

He wanted to know how much hardship there really was in Britain. Between 1889 and 1903 he studied the life of the poor in London and published his findings in 17 volumes published as *Life and Labour of the People in London*. His findings changed his opinion about the 'limited' levels of poverty in London. Booth concluded that 30% of London's population was living in poverty. Booth's work was important for a number of reasons:

- His method of working was important. He used scientific methods and put people into recognisable social classes.
- He worked out a 'poverty line'. (A level of income that was needed in order for a family to stay just beyond a life of starvation).
- He provided statistics that showed how widespread poverty was.
- The scale of the poverty he uncovered could not be met by charitable aid alone.

SOURCE 5.1

Population classification

A	The lowest class – occasional loafers, loafers and semi-criminals.
B	The very poor – casual labour, hand-to-mouth existence, chronic want.
C and D	The poor – including those whose earnings are small, because of irregularity of employment, and those whose work, though regular, is ill-paid.
E and F	The regularly employed and fairly-paid working class of all grades.
G and H	Lower and upper middle class and all above these levels.

SOURCE 5.2

The proportion of the different classes shown for all London are as follows:

A (lowest)	37,610	or	0.9 per cent	In poverty
B (very poor)	316,854	or	7.5 per cent	30.7 per cent
C and D (poor)	938,293	or	22.3 per cent	
E and F (working class, comfortable)	2,166,503	or	51.5 per cent	In comfort, 69.3 per cent
G and H (middle class and above)	749, 930	or	17.8 per cent	
Total	4,209,170		100 per cent	

Booth's findings were supported by another social investigator called Seebohm Rowntree. Rowntree was a member of a wealthy chocolate manufacturing family from York. A committed Christian, after reading Booth's work he decided to see if the level of poverty in York was different to that in London. In 1901 he published his book, *Poverty, A Study of Town Life*. His findings were similar to those of Booth.

Rowntree was important because:

◆ He showed that poverty was not just a problem in London. The York study proved that poverty was widespread. One third of the population living in towns lived in poverty.

◆ His study was also important because of the methods he used to carry out his study. Rowntree identified two types of poverty. *Primary poverty* was used to describe those people whose earnings were so low they could not survive on them alone. *Secondary poverty* was used to describe those whose earnings were enough to live on but who spent money in a wasteful way.

◆ He put a figure on the amount of money a worker needed to earn in order to maintain a family in a minimum standard of living.

SOURCE 5.3

From B S Rowntree, *Poverty, A Study of Town Life*.
Allowing for broken time, the average wage for a labourer in York is from 18s. to 21s.; whereas, according to the figures given earlier in this chapter, the minimum expenditure necessary to maintain in a state of physical efficiency a family of two adults and three children is 21s. 8d. or, if there are four children, the sum required would be 26s.

SOURCE 5.4

From B S Rowntree, *Poverty, A Study of Town Life*.
Let us clearly understand what 'merely physical efficiency' means. A family must never spend a penny on railway fare or omnibus. They must never purchase a halfpenny newspaper or spend a penny to buy a ticket for a popular concert. They must write no letters to absent children, for they cannot afford to pay the postage. They must never contribute anything to their church or chapel, or give any help to a neighbour which costs them money. They cannot save, nor can they join sick club or Trade Union, because they cannot pay the necessary subscriptions. The

children must have no pocket money for dolls, marbles, or sweets. The father must smoke no tobacco, and must drink no beer. The mother must never buy any pretty clothes for herself or for her children. ... Should a child fall ill, it must be attended by the parish doctor; should it die, it must be buried by the parish. Finally, the wage-earner must never be absent from his work for a single day.

These investigators of social conditions found that poverty was not always the fault of the person who was poor. Many of the elderly, the ill and those without work lived poor lives. However, many workers were paid wages so low, or were not paid regularly due to irregular work, that they could not afford life's basic needs. The poverty of these people was not their fault.

Booth and Rowntree were not professional researchers but they changed the way poverty was studied. They were very important men. Historians agree.

SOURCE 5.5

From J R Hay, *The Origins of the Liberal Reforms.*
The social surveys did tend to undermine the view that personal character deficiencies were the primary cause of poverty.

SOURCE 5.6

From D Fraser, *The Evolution of the British Welfare State.*
Booth and Rowntree gave to the growing public concern over poverty the statistical evidence on which to build the case for state aid.

Chapter summary

◆ Charles Booth and Seebohm Rowntree were private individuals who studied the amount of poverty in London and York.

◆ They brought new methods to study the amount of poverty that existed.

◆ Their findings showed that approximately 30% of the urban population in Britain, was living in poverty. This was the first time the scale of poverty had been calculated.

◆ Their findings showed that the amount of poverty that existed required levels of help that could only be provided by the British Government. Charity was not enough.

QUESTION PRACTICE

Intermediate 1

Source A was written by a historian called Theo Barker:

Poverty begins to attract more attention in this period primarily because men of social conscience, notably the shipowner Charles Booth and the chocolate manufacturer Seebohm Rowntree, began to investigate it, to quantify it and to reveal its reality and extent in irrefutable detail for the first time.

1 Use Source A and your own knowledge to explain why Charles Booth and Seebohm Rowntree are considered to be important by historians. *Outcome 2*

2 How useful is Source 5.2 for showing the extent of poverty in London in the 1890s? *Outcome 3*

Intermediate 2

1 Describe what Booth and Rowntree discovered about the causes of poverty. *Outcome 2*

6

THE BOER WAR AND CONCERNS FOR THE EMPIRE

In this chapter you will find out about:
- Why the Boer War worried people in Britain
- What National Efficiency means
- The Committee on Physical Deterioration

In 1899 war broke out between the powerful British Empire and the Boer Republics in South Africa. The Boers were descendents of Dutch settlers. The British thought that the war would be over quickly. Boer forces proved to be well trained, well equipped and well led. The war dragged on for three years. Eventually, Britain used 400,000 troops to defeat Boer forces that totalled 35,000. The war was a great shock to British confidence. In Britain people searched for answers as to why it had taken three years for professional soldiers to defeat a force of Boer farmers.

SOURCE 6.1

Photograph of wounded British soldiers outside a hospital during the Boer War.

The quality of soldiers was blamed for the poor British performance in the war. In some towns as many as nine out of ten recruits for the army were rejected because they were so unfit. In Source 6.3 Arnold White speaks about the numbers of recruits rejected in Manchester.

SOURCE 6.2

Map of Boer War.

The Boer War 1899-1902

ATLANTIC OCEAN

INDIAN OCEAN

Angola

German South West Africa

Walvis Bay

Southern Rhodesia

Portuguese East Africa

Lourenco Marques

Bechuanaland

Transvaal

Pretoria

Johannesburg

Vereening

Majuba Hill

Ladysmith

Natal

Durban

Bloemfontein

Vaal

Mafeking

Orange Free State

Kimberley

Magersfontein

Hope Town

De Aar

Cape Colony

Cape Town

British soldiers killed in battle	6,000
British died from wounds and disease	16,000
Total British dead	22,000
Boers killed in battle	4,000
Boer women and children who died in British concentration camps	9,000
Total Boer dead	13,000

0   200

Miles

1852 Convention recognises Boer independence in the Transvaal.
1881 Independence is again recognised by the Convention of Pretoria after the first Anglo-Boer War.
1902 Britain annexes Boer Republics after the Treaty of Vereening.
1910 Britain grants independence to the Union of South Africa, which remains within the British Commonwealth until becoming a republic in 1961

Key:
- British territory in 1858
- British expansion 1859-1885
- Boer campaigns 1899
- Towns besieged by Boers 1899-1900
- Main British advance 1900-1901
- Union of South Africa 1910

SOURCE 6.3

In the Manchester district 11,000 men offered themselves for war service between the outbreak of hostilities in October 1899 and July 1900. Of this number 8000 were found to be physically unfit to carry a rifle and stand the fatigues of discipline. Of the 3000 who were accepted only 1200 attained the moderate standard of muscular power and chest measurement required by the military authorities. In other words, two out of every three men willing to bear arms in the Manchester district are virtually invalids.

After the war, Major-General Sir Frederick Maurice in an article entitled, *National Health: A Soldier's Study*, complained that:

SOURCE 6.4

... out of every five men who wish to enlist and primarily offer themselves for enlistment you will find that by the end of two years' service there are only two men remaining in the Army as effective soldiers ...

Such figures were very worrying for a large Empire. They implied an unfit workforce as well as an unfit army. No wonder the British Army had performed so badly in South Africa and other countries were overtaking Britain in economic growth.

White blamed the conditions in Britain's towns. These conditions produced an unfit population. Such views were common at this time.

SOURCE 6.5

From A White, *Efficiency and Empire.*
A vast population has been created by the factory and industrial systems, the majority of which is incapable of bearing arms.
Spectacled school-children hungry, strumous, and epileptic, grow into consumptive bridegrooms and scrofulous brides.

Importantly, the Boer War was even further evidence that Britain was not doing enough to help the poorer in society.

SOURCE 6.6

From A Sykes, *The Rise and Fall of British Liberalism.*
The high proportion of army volunteers from the large towns rejected as physically unfit appeared to confirm the alarming findings of Booth and Rowntree.

People like Arnold White argued that the poor British economic performance (see Chapter 1) and the Boer War were proof of British decline. Their views were very common at this time. One response to this problem was to argue for social reforms. Social reform would make for a healthy population, which was more efficient as a workforce and as soldiers. This is often termed as arguing for National Efficiency.

One of the results of the Boer War was the setting up of a specially appointed *Committee on Physical Deterioration*. This was set up in 1903 to ask why so many army recruits were rejected because of their health. The Committee reported in 1904 that they

Chapter summary

1 The Boer War seemed to show that the population of Britain was unfit and unhealthy.
2 The number of unfit and unhealthy men was blamed for the 'decline' of the British Empire.
3 In order for Britain's population to become more 'efficient', social reforms were proposed.

had found no evidence of long-term physical deterioration of the population in Britain, but they made many recommendations including medical inspection of children in schools, free school meals for the very poor, and training in mother craft.

These conclusions were very important in the future Liberal Reforms.

The importance of the Boer War is huge according to the historian Eric Evans:

SOURCE 6.7

Arguably, the single most important precondition for the spate of social reforms between 1905 and 1914 was fear of the consequences of an unfit and debilitated population.

7

WHY DID ATTITUDES TOWARDS POVERTY CHANGE? POLITICAL DEVELOPMENTS IN BRITAIN

In this chapter you will find out:
- When more working-class men got the vote
- Why working-class voters supported the Labour Party
- Why the Liberal Party began to think about social reform

Throughout the 19th century there were political developments that made reform of the help given to the poor an important issue. By 1900 these developments had led to the emergence of a new political force called the Labour Representation Committee. This was renamed the Labour Party in 1906.

DEMOCRATIC DEVELOPMENTS

After reforms in 1867 and 1884, the number of men who could vote in General Elections increased. Six out of ten men had the vote. This meant that by 1890 the majority of people voting were members of the working class. The working class could now elect people who wanted to change the way Britain was run and wanted to pass reforms that would help the working class.

THE DEVELOPMENT OF TRADE UNIONISM

Throughout the 19th century, membership of Trade Unions had grown. Between 1892 and 1900 membership had grown from 1.6 million to just over 2 million members. Unions had changed from being small unions that represented skilled craft workers to larger 'new' unions that represented unskilled and semi-skilled workers. In the 1890s there were several big strikes and lockouts. This led unions to look to Parliament to protect them from unemployment and employers. This led to Trade Union support for a new Labour Party, which would help them. Many people in the Trade Union movement felt that the Liberals and Conservatives did not do enough to help ordinary working-class people.

"WORKLESS"

SOURCE 7.1

Labour Party election poster from the 1910 elections. The poster drew attention to the political issue of the unemployed.

THE SPREAD OF SOCIALISM AND SOCIALIST IDEAS

By the 1890s there had been a growth in Socialist thinking. Socialists argued that the Government of Britain should interfere more with the way the country was organised. The Government had the power to change the country by passing laws. Many socialists felt very strongly about the levels of poverty in Britain.

SOURCE 7.2

George Bernard Shaw, a famous playwright and socialist, said, in a speech delivered at the War Against Poverty Demonstration, organised by the Independent Labour Party and the Fabian Society in the Albert Hall, London, 11 October 1912:

I want to cure poverty as an abominable disease and as a very horrible crime.

The Labour Party started to grow slowly. Working-class voters had traditionally voted for the Liberal Party. They continued to do so for some time.

SOURCE 7.3

General election results for Labour
1900: 2 MPs
1906: 29 MPs
1910 (Jan): 40 MPs
1910 (Dec): 42 MPs

Labour stood for practical reforms to tackle poverty. Labour Manifesto from 1906 appealed for action saying:

SOURCE 7.4

The aged poor are neglected
The slums remain: overcrowding continues, while the land goes to waste.

Wars are fought to make the rich richer, and underfed school children are still neglected.

The unemployed ask for work, the Government gave them a worthless Act and now the red herring of protection is drawn across your path.

Production, as experience shows, is no remedy for poverty and unemployment. It seems to keep you from dealing with the land, housing, old age and other social problems.

You have in your power to see that Parliament carries out your wishes. The Labour Representation Executive appeals to you in the name of a million Trade Unionists.

The emergence of the Labour Party and their quest to end poverty pressurised the Liberal Party. It threatened to take away the support they had among working-class voters. This encouraged the Liberal Party to think hard about social reform.

LIBERAL THINKING

Traditionally, Liberals had supported theories of self-help and minimal state involvement in running society. By the 1900s some Liberal thinkers were thinking that this had failed and supported state interference. These New Liberals argued that self-help had not worked. The state should become involved in helping people instead.

SOURCE 7.5

From LT Hobhouse, *Liberalism*.

In the earlier days of the Free Trade era, it was permissible to hope that the average workman would be able by the exercise of prudence and thrift to maintain himself in good times, but to lay by for sickness, unemployment, and old age. The course of events has in large measure disappointed these hopes. It is true that the standard of living in England has progressively advanced throughout the nineteenth century ... yet there appears <u>no likelihood</u> that the average manual worker will attain the goal of that full independence, covering all the risks of life for self and family.

By the early 20th century, problems in Britain were so great that the state had to take a role in improving standards of living for its citizens. The scale of poverty identified by Booth and Rowntree had been shocking. Political thinking and new voters also demanded such a change. The state was going to increase its role in organising society in order to improve it. It was the Liberal Party that would begin to tackle the huge poverty that existed in Britain.

Chapter summary

◆ By the 1890s the increased number of working-class voters and their concerns led to the emergence of the Labour Party.

◆ The Labour Party stood for policies that appealed to working-class voters. Reform to deal with poverty was important to them.

◆ The Liberal Party also began to argue that the state had a role to play in dealing with the problems of society.

QUESTION PRACTICE

Intermediate 1

Source A

Philip Snowden, a leading member of the Labour Party, called on voters in 1900, to:

Come with us and help us to remove poverty, sin, and suffering, and to bring hope, and health, and joy, and brotherhood to every child of our common Father

from the Northern Daily Telegraph, 26 September, 1900

1 In what ways did the Labour Party attract support from working-class voters?

Outcome 1

Intermediate 2

1 Why did the Labour Party threaten the Liberal Party's traditional support from working-class voters?

Outcome 2

8 THE LIBERAL GOVERNMENT, 1906–14

THE LIBERAL GOVERNMENT

In 1906 a General Election gave the Liberal Party a huge majority in Parliament. The final results were as follows:

Conservative:	157 MPs
Liberal:	400 MPs
Labour:	29 MPs
Irish Nationalist:	82 MPs

NEW LIBERALISM

The Liberal Government was first led by Henry Campbell-Bannerman until his death in 1908. Herbert Asquith then became Prime Minister from 1908. Within the Liberal Party were a group of politicians who were very interested in the problem of poverty. They are known as New Liberals. They emerged as a direct response to the evidence of poverty, bad diet, poor housing and lack of education that had been revealed by people like Rowntree and Booth. The two most important New Liberals in the Government were Winston Churchill and David Lloyd George. These politicians were willing to use the power of the state to intervene in society and try to end poverty. They did this for a number of reasons.

FACTFILE

Winston Churchill (1874–1965) is forever remembered as a war leader during the Second World War. He had an interesting career before this. Churchill had been a war correspondent during the Boer War. In the 1900 General Election, Churchill was elected as a Conservative MP. In 1904 he joined the Liberal Party after reading Rowntree's study of poverty in York. He became very interested in social reform as a result. In 1908 Churchill was President of the Board of Trade. While in this post he carried through important social legislation including the establishment of employment exchanges. Churchill became Home Secretary in 1910, then First Lord of the Admiralty in 1911. In 1922 he rejoined the Conservative Party and in 1940 became Prime Minister.

Churchill's response to seeing Rowntree's study of poverty was to say:

SOURCE 8.1

I see little glory in an Empire which can rule the waves and is unable to flush its sewers.

Churchill had a genuine concern for the poor and the conditions in which they lived. In a speech at St Andrew's Hall, Glasgow, 11 October 1906. He said:

SOURCE 8.2

The cause of the Liberal Party is the cause of the left-out millions.

Churchill also saw social reform as a way of undermining the Labour Party.

SOURCE 8.3

From A Sykes, *the Rise and Fall of British Liberalism.*
Churchill saw social reform not only as desirable in itself, but as a policy which would revive the flagging fortunes of the party.

FACTFILE

David Lloyd George, 1863–1945. Lloyd George was born in Manchester but was brought up in North Wales by his uncle, Richard Lloyd. In 1890 he was elected as Liberal MP of Caernarvon. He was a brilliant public speaker. He was president of the Board of Trade (1905–1908) then Chancellor of the Exchequer (1908–1915). His own father had died due to ill health. He was committed to social reform and was very important in bringing in Old Age Pensions and the National Insurance Act. It was Lloyd George who led the battle against the House of Lords for the Liberal Party. Lloyd George became Prime Minster between 1916 and 1922.

SOURCE 8.4

Lloyd George speech at Manchester, 1908:
After all, this is a rich country. It is the richest country under the sun; and yet in this rich country you have hundreds and thousands of people living under conditions of poverty, destitution, and squalor that would, in the words of an old Welsh poet, make the rocks weep.

Churchill and Lloyd George were very important in leading the Liberal reforms. At the time they were seen as being very enthusiastic politicians. Maybe they were a little too enthusiastic according to the following cartoon.

SOURCE 8.5

Lloyd George as a young man.

Chapter summary

◆ The Liberal Government were elected with a large majority in 1906.

◆ The Liberal Government had 'New' Liberals who were very interested in social reform.

◆ The two important government ministers who were especially interested in social reform were Winston Churchill and David Lloyd George.

"SUPPORTERS" RAMPANT.

AN HERALDIC INVERSION.

SOURCE 8.6

Cartoon showing Asquith, the Prime Minister balancing his two enthusiastic Ministers on his shoulders. The cartoonist thinks that Asquith was embarrassed by the speeches of Lloyd George and Winston Churchill.

QUESTION PRACTICE

For Intermediate 2 you will have to write some longer answers. They are called Extended Answers.

Your extended answer is worth 8 marks.

1 What were the main reasons for changing attitudes towards poverty before 1906?

Since this is your first 8-mark essay you will find advice about doing this question on pages 103 and 104.

9 THE LIBERAL REFORMS: CHILDREN

In this chapter you will find out about:
- Meals and medical inspections for children (1906 and 1907 Acts)
- The Children's Charter (1908)

MEALS FOR CHILDREN

WHY WAS THIS ACT PASSED?

The first reform passed by the Liberal Government that attacked the problem of poverty was the provision of school meals for poor children. The Boer War and the poor condition of many recruits led politicians to act. The children were the soldiers of the future. Healthy children would grow up to be healthy soldiers and workers. The British Empire would be stronger as a result.

In December 1906, the Education (provision of meals) Act was passed. The Liberal Government had supported a Bill introduced by a Labour Member of Parliament. This shows the importance of the new Labour MPs even at this early stage.

THE ACT

- It allowed local education authorities to provide school meals for poor children.
- It allowed local authorities to raise a local tax (called a rate) to pay for this.
- Children who were from better-off families were expected to pay for their food.

To begin with, the Act was not a success. The Act was voluntary which meant that many local authorities chose not to provide food for the children. By 1913 over half the education authorities in England and Wales had not begun to provide school meals.

The problem was money. The government helped in 1914 by providing money to meet half the cost of the meals.

WHY IS THIS ACT IMPORTANT?

- By providing school meals for poor children the Government was feeding the children rather than their families. This challenged the idea of self-help.

SOURCE 9.1

As the historian Derek Fraser says:

the state was little by little acknowledging responsibility for the sick, the unemployed and the hungry. As always, from little things great developments grow.

◆ It was very difficult to say who deserved a school meal. More children than expected were given meals as a result. It was also difficult to make parents pay for the meals, so they were provided free to all children.

There were objections to this act. It was argued that providing school meals was expensive. Maybe more important was the following argument provided by Sir Arthur Clay. He objected to providing school meals because:

SOURCE 9.2

to feed a child is to give relief to its parents and the effect must be to undermine their independence and self-reliance, and to give their children an object-lesson in the evasion of responsibility which will never be forgotten, and which will bear fruit when they in their turn become parents.

MEDICAL INSPECTIONS FOR CHILDREN

WHY WAS THIS ACT PASSED?

The need for a healthy Britain also led to the medical inspection of children. This had been recommended by the Report of the Physical Deterioration Committee in 1904. This Committee had been set up to look at the reasons why Britain performed badly in the Boer War. The reasoning behind this provision was therefore similar to the provision for the school meals.

In 1907 an Education Bill was passed. Part of this Bill introduced the school medical inspection of children.

The inspectors identified the problem very well. Doctors produced many reports on the poor health of children. What the reform did not do was provide treatment for the illnesses. To deal with this problem, many clinics were introduced into schools to provide treatment. From 1912 the Government provided help to pay for these clinics.

WHY IS THIS ACT IMPORTANT?

◆ The state had taken another big step towards looking after its citizens; in this case, children.
◆ The theory of 'self-help' was again being attacked.
◆ Such actions were seen as a small step towards greater healthcare for all people in Britain.

SOURCE 9.3

From Derek Fraser, *The Evolution of the Britsih Welfare State.*
Another step had been taken towards a general medical service.

SOURCE 9.4

A medical inspection of schoolchildren taking place. The hair is being checked for vermin.

THE CHILDREN'S CHARTER, 1908

The 1908 Children's Act was the creation of a Liberal Member of Parliament called Herbert Samuel. The Act brought together many earlier laws such as the Prevention of Cruelty to Children's Act of 1889, and produced one Law, which covered all aspects of care for children.

THE ACT

The Children's Act clearly stated what the legal rights of children were:

♦ If children were not cared for properly by their parents, the community (in reality the Government) should care for them.
♦ Children were banned from buying cigarettes under the age of 16 and were not allowed in public houses under the age of 14.
♦ It was forbidden to give alcohol to children under the age of five, except in the case of illness.
♦ It allowed for the inspection of children's homes.
♦ It ordered parents to guard their fires because 1,000 little children were burnt to death every year.
♦ Child criminals were not to be sent to prisons with adult prisoners any more. The Act set up special Juvenile Courts and the borstal system.
♦ The death sentence for children was abolished.

WHY IS THIS ACT IMPORTANT?

♦ The Act is important because it protected children from abuse.
♦ Responsibility for children and how they were being brought up was being regulated by the state. Again, self-help was being challenged.'
♦ It is often called the Children's 'Charter' because it covered so many aspects of life for children.

Chapter summary
♦ School meals were brought in for the poor but many local authorities did not provide them due to cost.
♦ Medical inspection of children was introduced. This identified the problem rather than provided a cure.
♦ The Children's Charter provided legal protection for children.
♦ All these Acts were important in showing how the state was increasing its role in the lives of children. Some people argued that this took responsibility away from the parents.

QUESTION PRACTICE

Intermediate 1

Source A is from the Report of the Inter-Departmental Committee on Physical Deterioration (HMSO, 1904), Cd. 2175, I, 84–93.

(41) Medical inspection of school children
The Committee are emphatic in recommending that a systematised medical inspection of children at school should be imposed as a public duty on every school authority ...
(42) Feeding of elementary school children.
The Committee recommend that definite provision should be made by the various Local Authorities for dealing with the question of underfed children ...

1 Using Source A and your own knowledge, explain why the medical inspection of school children and the feeding of school children was introduced by the Liberals. *Outcome 2*

2 What is the value of Source A for someone studying this topic? *Outcome 3*

Intermediate 2

1 In what ways did the Liberal Reforms help children to escape from poverty? *Outcome 1*

2 How useful is Source 9.2 in showing opposition to the introduction of school meals for children? *Outcome 3*

10 THE LIBERAL REFORMS: THE ELDERLY AND OLD AGE PENSIONS (1908)

In this chapter you will find out:
- Why Old Age Pensions were introduced
- What Old Age Pensions were paid
- About the effects of pensions
- About the problems this measure produced for the Government

The Social Investigator Charles Booth had shown how much poverty was due to old age. Once people had stopped working they did not earn money. Under the theory of 'self-help' such people should have saved money for this time. All the evidence was that many elderly people simply could not afford to save when they worked. They did not earn enough money. The families of old people could not always afford to look after them. Such elderly people often found themselves in the workhouse under the Poor Law system. This was considered humiliating by people like Booth who supported the introduction of pensions as a way of making sure that old people had money to live independently, later on in life.

In 1895 Booth gave evidence to the Royal Commission on the Aged Poor, where he proposed the introduction of a pension scheme:

SOURCE 10.1

Charles Booth:
On the scheme that I wish to bring before the Commission it is intended that every one born in England or Wales ... shall, when 65, be entitled to the pension ... of 5s. a week.

There was a lot of support for Old Age Pensions. Pressure for reform came from a number of places.
- Most people thought that pension payments for the elderly were a good idea.
- Government Commissions such as *The Royal Commission on the Aged Poor*, 1895 had provided evidence, which supported the idea of pensions for the elderly.
- Countries such as New Zealand and Germany had already introduced pensions for the elderly by 1906.
- The Labour Party and Trade Unions supported the introduction of pensions.
- Although the Liberals were very interested in stopping poverty they had other reasons for introducing pensions. By 1908 they were losing seats in Parliament to the Labour Party in a series of by-elections. It was believed by some in the Liberal Party that a measure, which was supported by many working-class voters, would make them more likely to vote Liberal in the future.

SOURCE 10.2

Lloyd George himself said:

It is time we did something that appealed straight to the people – it will, I think, help to stop this electoral rot and that is most necessary.

The Act was guided through the House of Commons by The Chancellor of the Exchequer, David Lloyd George.

THE ACT

- The pension was to be paid for from general taxation. No contributions had to be made by those who received the pension.
- The pension was paid to people over 70 years of age.
- When paid at the full rate, the pension was worth 5 shillings a week to a single person and 10 shillings a week for a married couple.
- The amount of money paid as a pension varied depending on how much money the elderly had. Savings could be used to provide an income.
- Payments were to be made through the Post Office. The hated Poor Law was not used.

SOURCE 10.3

The pension was paid to people over 70 years old.

	Pension per week
Where yearly means are no greater in value than £21	5 s
Where yearly means are greater in value than £21 but no greater than:	
£23 12s 6d	4s
£26 5s 0d	3s
£28 17s 6d	2s
£31 10s 0d	1s
Pension for a married couple	10s

WHY IS THIS ACT IMPORTANT?

- Old people did not have to make contributions to qualify for payments of Old Age Pensions. Again the self-help principle of saving for old age had been broken.

As Lloyd George said during a Parliamentary debate on the subject:

SOURCE 10.5

Payments are made to the elderly at a post office.

THE NEW YEAR'S GIFT.

SOURCE 10.7

A child bringing the gift of Old Age Pensions to an elderly couple. Pensions helped to free many poor people over the age of 70 from having to ask for help.

SOURCE 10.4

Let me give now two or three considerations why, in my judgment, a contributory scheme is impossible in this country. In the first place, it would practically exclude women from its benefits. Out of the millions of members of friendly societies there is but a small proportion of women. Another is that the vast majority are not earning anything and cannot pay their contributions. The second reason is that the majority of working men are unable to deflect from their weekly earnings a sufficient sum of money to make adequate provision for old age in addition to that which they are now making for sickness, infirmity, and unemployment.

♦ Payment of pensions was made through the Post Office where other business, such as selling stamps, took place. People were not branded as poor when they went to the Post Office, unlike if they went to the workhouse. Many more people claimed the pension as a result.

♦ The amount of money on offer was not enough to live on, on its own. It 'topped up' the income that elderly people already had. It made a real difference to many.

♦ The demand for pensions was higher than expected. The Government had planned for expenditure of £6.5 million on pensions. They cost £8 million in the first year. This caused problems for the Government as they had to find this extra money from somewhere.

The Manchester Guardian newspaper reported the first payment of pensions:

SOURCE 10.6

The first payments under the Old-age Pensions Act were made yesterday at post-offices ... probably about half a million needy old people were made glad yesterday by the first instalment of an allowance which will be continued to them for the rest of their lives, and it is not surprising to read that many of the recipients expressed heartfelt thanks to the willing instruments of the State's bounty — the post-office clerks who handed them their money.

Chapter summary

◆ Many different groups agreed that Old Age Pensions were a good idea.

◆ Old Age Pensions were paid to people over the age of 70.

◆ Payments were made from taxation. No contribution had to be made.

◆ The Act was popular and cost more money than the Government thought it would.

THE PHILANTHROPIC HIGHWAYMAN.

Mr. Lloyd-George. *"I'LL MAKE 'EM PITY THE AGED POOR!"*

SOURCE 10.8

Punch magazine's famous cartoon of Lloyd George demanding money to pay for his Old Age Pensions.

QUESTION PRACTICE

Intermediate 1

Source A In her village Flora Thompson saw the reaction to Pensions:

When old age pensions began life was transformed for aged cottagers. They were relieved of anxiety. They were suddenly rich. Independent for life! At first when they went to the Post Office tears of gratitude would run down the cheeks of some and they would say as they picked up their money, 'God bless that Lord George and God bless you, miss' and there were flowers from their gardens and apples from the trees for the girls who merely handed them the money.

1 Using Source A and your own knowledge, describe the effects of the introduction of Old Age Pensions.

Outcome 1

2 Why is Source A useful as evidence of the reaction to the payment of Old Age Pensions? *Outcome 3*

Intermediate 2

1 Use Source 10.2 and your own knowledge to explain why Old Age Pensions were introduced, by the Liberal Government, in 1908. *Outcome 2*

2 How useful is Source 10.7 to someone studying this topic?

PROBLEMS FOR THE LIBERAL REFORM PROGRAMME

Pensions cost the Government much more money than they had been expecting to pay. At the same time Britain had to find the money to fund a shipbuilding programme caused by the launch of HMS Dreadnought in 1906 and rivalry with Germany over trade and colonies. The Government needed to find more money to pay for this expenditure. This meant that the people of Britain would have to pay more in the way of taxes.

THE BUDGET OF 1909

The person in charge of the finances of the country was the Chancellor of the Exchequer, Lloyd George. He needed to raise £16 million to pay for pensions and ships. He proposed to do this by the following:

SOURCE 11.1

* Increasing the tax paid on the income people earned. This would range from 9d to 1s 2d in the pound depending on how much you earned. The better off, who had been paying 1s, were targeted with increases.
* Introducing a super tax of 6d in the pound which was put on incomes over £3,000.
* Introducing higher taxes (called duties) which were placed on tobacco, beer, spirits and petrol.
* Introducing a land tax of 20% paid when land changed hands on the unearned increase in land value.
* Introducing a duty of ½d in the pound on the value of undeveloped land and minerals (this measure meant that a complete valuation of land in Britain would be needed.)

Lloyd George thought this budget was very important. When he made a speech to Parliament on the budget he said:

SOURCE 11.2

This is a War Budget. It is for raising money to wage implacable warfare against poverty and squalidness.

The budget wanted to increase taxes for the rich in society. In particular, Lloyd George targeted wealthy land-owners. These taxes were then to be spent on helping the poorer in society. This use of taxes involves what is called a 'redistribution of wealth'. In 1909 many Conservatives did not like these proposals. In the House of Commons the Conservatives were outnumbered by the Liberals but in the House of Lords the Conservatives held a majority. Many of the Conservative Lords were land-owners who were very annoyed at the proposals to pay taxes on their land. In November 1909 they rejected the Budget by 350 votes to 75.

The Liberal Government was faced with a crisis. Who was in control of Britain they argued? Was it the House of Commons who were elected, or the aristocratic House of Lords?

The Liberals attacked the House of Lords for not listening to the views of the majority of people in Britain. They were shown as men who wanted wealth for themselves and were willing to let the people of Britain down. Lloyd George attacked the Lords, saying:

SOURCE 11.3

Should 500 men, ordinary men chosen accidentally from among the unemployed [a reference to the fact that many of the lords did not work due to their wealth], *override the judgment – the deliberate judgment – of millions of people who are engaged in the industry which makes the wealth of the country?*

he continued

who made 10,000 people [a reference to the number of land-owners in Britain] *the owners of the soil, and the rest of us trespassers in the land of our birth.*

RICH FARE.

THE GIANT LLOYD-GORGIBUSTER: "FEE, FI, FO, FAT,
I SMELL THE BLOOD OF A PLUTOCRAT;
BE HE ALIVE OR BE HE DEAD,
I'LL GRIND HIS BONES TO MAKE MY BREAD."

SOURCE 11.4

Cartoon from Punch magazine showing Lloyd George chasing a rich man (Plutocrat) in order to pay for his tax increases.

The Liberal Prime Minister, Herbert Asquith, called an election over the *'People's Budget'* as the Liberals called it, in January 1910. The Liberals won a majority with their allies in the Labour Party and Irish Nationalists. The Budget proposals were passed by the House of Lords and became law, after this victory.

The Liberals now continued to fight to make sure that the House of Lords could never again threaten laws passed by the House of Commons. A second election was held in December. The Liberals and their allies won again. The King threatened to create a Liberal majority in the Lords if it did not pass the Parliament Bill. After this threat the Parliament Act was passed in 1911. The House of Lords could no longer stop laws passed by the House of Commons.

SOURCE 11.5

The two elections of 1910:

January 1910		December 1910	
Liberals	275	Liberals	272
Labour	40	Labour	42
Irish Nationalists	82	Irish Nationalists	84
Conservatives	273	Conservatives	272

The Parliament Act said that:
- The House of Lords could only delay legislation passed by the House of Commons for two years, not reject it.
- The House of Lords could not delay finance bills (the Budget).

The social reform programme could continue without opposition from the Lords.

Chapter summary
- Old Age Pensions cost more than the Government had calculated for.
- The Government also had to pay for a programme of Naval Warship building.
- The budget to pay for these was rejected by the House of Lords.
- After a long struggle, the power of the House of Lords was reduced by the Parliament Act 1911.

12 THE LIBERAL REFORMS: HEALTH

After the defeat of the House of Lords, Lloyd George and Churchill looked to expand the reform programme. Lloyd George in particular wanted to help more people than just children and the elderly. He also wanted to help those who became poor through ill health and unemployment. He was especially interested in those affected by ill health. Bad health cost many workers their jobs, and eventually their lives. Lloyd George's own father had been a victim of tuberculosis which claimed 75,000 lives a year at this time. Benefits for those who were sick were provided for in Part I of the National Insurance Act of 1911.

WHAT WAS INSURANCE?

Lloyd George was aware that Old Age Pensions had been far more expensive than the Government had thought they would be. The Insurance scheme planned allowed employer, employee (worker) and state to contribute money to a fund of money when the worker was employed, or in good health. When the worker was ill, or became unemployed, amounts of money were paid out to the worker for a limited period of time. This money was to help the worker through a difficult period when they could have fallen into poverty.

Insurance was popular to the Liberals as a way of paying for reforms because:
- Insurance meant the cost of reform was not too expensive for the Government.
- It allowed workers to make contributions for their own care. This was considered to give workers a sense of pride as they were not getting 'something for nothing'. It made the scheme 'respectable'.
- A similar system, that covered health, had been working well in Germany since the 1880s.

It was also hoped that grateful workers would vote Liberal in return for the help provided.

There was a lot of opposition to the reform from:
- Friendly Societies who ran their own schemes to save for times when workers were ill.
- Trade Unions who objected to the fact that working men were being expected to contribute to the reform.
- Private Insurance Companies such as the Prudential which felt threatened by the scheme proposed by the Government.

♦ The House of Lords which attempted to delay the reform.
♦ Doctors who worried about the role of the state. The head of the British Medical Association attacked it. He said that it stopped individuals making an effort and would cost too much money to run.

In the face of such opposition Lloyd George was forced into a number of actions.

♦ He had to abandon benefits for widows and orphans. This won over the big insurance companies.
♦ The Friendly Societies were won over by administering the State Scheme.

In 1911 the National Insurance Act was passed. It had two parts. Part I dealt with sickness (see below) and Part II dealt with unemployment benefit (see Chapter 13).

SOURCE 12.1

The National Insurance Act: Part I: Sickness Benefit.
Payments:
♦ Employees contributed 4d a week if they earned under £160 a year.
♦ Employers contributed 3d a week.
♦ The state contributed 2d a week.
♦ Contributions were recorded by placing stamps on cards.

It gave workers '9d for 3d' in contributions according to Lloyd George.
Benefits:
♦ Insured workers were entitled to 10 shillings a week for 13 weeks and 5 shillings for another 13 weeks if ill.
♦ Insured workers were entitled to free medical treatment from a doctor chosen by a local Insurance Commission.
♦ Insured workers were entitled to 30 shillings maternity benefit for the birth of each child.

SOURCE 12.2

Government poster showing what was paid and the benefit received.

Problems of the reform:

◆ After using up their 26 week entitlement, ill workers had to rely on the Poor Law medical facilities.
◆ Only the person who earned money was entitled to these benefits. The family got no benefits if they fell ill.
◆ The self-employed, unemployed and those already covered by private health insurance were not included.
◆ Many people objected to licking the stamps.

Some felt that the reform did not go far enough. The Labour Member of Parliament, Keir Hardie thought that a married woman should get the same benefits as the husband because her sickness would have the same bad effect on the family.

SOURCE 12.4

… the relief that is proposed to be given to the bread winner under this Bill will, to a certain extent, relieve the pressure which inevitably follows a period of sickness. But that pressure is not felt alone in the time when the breadwinner himself is disabled. When the wife is sick, it is nearly always necessary to pay for outside help, which has to be brought in. The married woman requires nursing, the housework requires to be done, young children require to be looked after, and it entails extra expenditure, which the wages of the husband makes it impossible for him to adequately meet.

Effects of the reform:

◆ Again the state had extended its role to help the poor in society. The Act was a compulsory one.
◆ The Act was not always appreciated by those it was intended to help. Many workers were angry at being forced to contribute money from their wages to this fund. It reduced the size of their wage packet. The Liberals did not get the electoral benefits they hoped for. In fact, the Insurance Act was blamed for the loss of at least two seats in Parliament as angry workers voted for other political parties before 1914.
◆ Once your entitlement had been used up the ill worker had to go to the Poor Law.

SOURCE 12.3

A cartoon in Punch magazine that shows how mistresses and maids objected to the 'stamp-licking' proposals of the Insurance Bill. The punch bag has Lloyd George's face on it.

THE COMING OLYMPIC STRUGGLE.
Active Training for the Passive Resistance Event.

Chapter summary

◆ Health Insurance required contributions from employee, employer and the state. Benefits were paid out when enough contributions had been made.
◆ Health Insurance provided cover for the person contributing. The rest of the family was not covered in the event of ill health.
◆ Health Insurance saw the Government taking more responsibility for looking after people in Britain.

QUESTION PRACTICE

Intermediate 1

1 Use Source 12.2 to describe the main parts of The National Insurance Act (Part I: Health). *Outcome 1*

Intermediate 2

Source A

Snowden, an important Labour MP commented on the National Insurance Bill in 1911.

I am quite sure if this Bill passes into law the compulsory deduction every week from the wages of workmen will be very much resented.

1 Using Source A and your own knowledge, explain why many people did not like the National Insurance Act. *Outcome 2*

2 What is the value of Source 12.3 to someone studying this topic? *Outcome 3*

13 LIBERAL REFORMS: EMPLOYMENT REFORM

The Liberal Government tried to improve working conditions in some jobs. The jobs that they tried to improve were either dangerous or poorly paid. Low pay had been identified as a cause of poverty. They also tried to improve the conditions for workers who were not employed regularly. Irregular work had also been identified as a cause of poverty. These workers were to be helped find new jobs and given limited help if they became unemployed.

The Acts that were passed to help improve working conditions included:

1908	Mines Act	Mining was a dangerous job. This Act limited the length of time that a miner could work, to eight hours a day.
1909	Trade Boards Act	Boards were established in so called 'sweated' trades such as tailoring, box-making and lace-making. Such trades had long hours and little pay. The boards negotiated minimum wages for those who worked in such trades.
1911	Shops Act	This Act limited the hours that shop-workers worked, to 60 hours a week. This Act also made shops close for half a day in the week. This gave shop-workers time off.

Also of concern to the Liberals was unemployment. Government ministers like Churchill were particularly worried by short-term unemployment. This sort of unemployment was when workers had work, but only for fixed periods of time. Between these times they had no work and often no money to live on, as they could not save enough. Such workers were not covered by insurance schemes run by trade unions and could not contribute to the schemes run by friendly societies.

When he became President of the Board of Trade, Winston Churchill was introduced to a man called William Beveridge. Beveridge had ideas on how the problem of unemployment could be solved. He was employed by the Board of Trade, where Churchill was heavily influenced by his ideas. Beveridge and Churchill believed that the solution to short-term unemployment was to come in two ways.

MEASURE I: LABOUR EXCHANGES

In 1908 the Labour Exchange Act was passed and on the 1 February, 1910, 83 labour exchanges opened their doors across the country. Winston Churchill visited 17 on the first day they opened. They were run by Government officials. The idea behind a labour exchange was that unemployed workers could go there to find work. Employers would also go to these exchanges in order to find workers if they needed to. The idea was a good one and the number of exchanges grew quickly. By 1911 there were 414 exchanges in operation helping workers find jobs.

There were a number of problems, however.
* The scheme was voluntary.
* Employers did not have to tell the exchanges they had vacancies.
* Workers did not have to register with the exchanges if they were out of work.

Exchanges also offered a place for workers to mend their clothes and washing facilities for them to get clean. These exchanges seem to have been used by skilled workers and employers who needed such people. The manual and casual labourer were less likely to become involved. Can you think why?

MEASURE II: THE 1911 NATIONAL INSURANCE ACT PART II: UNEMPLOYMENT BENEFIT

As with the health insurance, employer, employee and the state were to make weekly contributions into a fund of money. Once a worker had contributed enough they had the right to withdraw money from this fund in the event of becoming unemployed.

The insurance principle was again applied. It was cheaper to fund benefits in this way and the worker was supposed to be grateful as he was contributing to his own benefit scheme.

SOURCE 13.1

Workers looking for jobs at one of the first labour exchanges at Camberwell in England.

SOURCE 13.2

The National Insurance Act: Part II: Unemployment benefit payments:
* Employees contributed 2½d per week.
* Employers contributed 2½d per week.
* The state contributed 1⅔d per week.

Benefits:
* In the event of becoming unemployed the benefit was 7 shillings a week for up to 15 weeks.
* A week's benefit was paid, for every five weeks of contributions made.
* Benefit was administered through the Labour Exchanges.

Problems of the reform:
* There was no cover for the rest of the family – only the person making the contributions.

National Insurance Act.

I've been to the butchers for a tongue to lick my stamps.

THIS STAMP WILL TAKE A BIT OF
LICKING

"Reg. and Copyright applied for

SOURCE 13.5

The Act was very important. These postcards were produced in support of the National Insurance Act.

◆ It only provided limited cover if the worker was unemployed. Once the entitlement had been used up the Poor Law had to be used.

The measure was intended to be limited. In the debate on the reform, the minister introducing it said:

SOURCE 13.3

The benefits are strictly limited in duration and to a large extent proportionate to the contributions.

◆ The reform was never intended to cover all types of unemployment. It only applied to a limited number of industries: building, mechanical engineering, shipbuilding, iron founding, saw milling and vehicle construction. These were industries that employed workers for short periods of time but then made them unemployed when the work had finished. The workers in such industries were frequently skilled. The Act was intended purely to help the worker between jobs. The trades that had to contribute to the scheme were building, construction, shipbuilding, mechanical engineering, iron founding, vehicle construction and saw milling. Only 2,250,000 men were covered against unemployment. Again, this was intentional:

SOURCE 13.4

The House may ask why particular classes (trades) are in fact chosen. The trades to which I have referred are the trades in which we found, on the whole, that the fluctuations of employment were the greatest and, on the whole, they were the trades most sensitive to ups and downs of depression and good times.

Significance of the reform:
◆ The scheme was highly original. No equivalent scheme had been introduced anywhere else in the world.
◆ No distinction was made between deserving and undeserving cases, further undermining ideas of individual self-help.
◆ Again the role of the state and what it took responsibility for was extended.
◆ The Act recognised that unemployment had complex causes.

The passage of the Insurance Bill had been a difficult one and opposition to the overall reform continued in parts of the country after it had become law. Protests in Aberdeen and the North East of Scotland took place over many years.

The National Insurance Act came into operation on the 15 July, 1912.

Date	Event
29 Nov 1911	Aberdeen Employees protest against the Insurance Bill.
Oct 1911	Aberdeen Doctors threaten strike against Insurance scheme.
1912	Many meetings in Aberdeenshire against the Insurance Scheme.
31 Aug 1912	Anti Insurance Act demonstration at Turriff, Aberdeenshire.
Aug 1912	Anti Insurance Act demonstration (with burning of effigy) at Inverurie, Aberdeenshire.
25 Aug 1913	Turriff protest meeting against the Insurance Act.
25 Aug 1913	Ellon protest meeting against the Insurance Act.
8 Dec 1913	Rioting against the Insurance Act in Turriff. A local farmer, Robert Paterson, had refused to pay his contributions to the Insurance Scheme. In order to pay for his contribution Insurance Commissioners seized one of his cows and tried to sell it in Turriff. The cow was unsold and rioting was the result.
16 Dec 1913	Turriff 'Insurance' cow sold in Aberdeen.
6–10 Jan 1914	Turriff Insurance Riots Trial in Aberdeen. Charges against eight accused were found to be 'not proven'. Robert Paterson was fined £15 for not paying £7 worth of National Insurance stamps for Employees. He refused to pay the fine as he believed that, as farm servants, his workers were never unemployed and seldom ill. Therefore both they and he should not be forced to pay National Insurance Contributions.

Chapter summary
- The Liberals passed reforms that helped reduce the hours of work and guaranteed minimum levels of pay in certain jobs.
- Labour Exchanges were opened to help unemployed men to find jobs. The Exchanges were popular but mostly used by skilled labourers.
- The National Insurance Act (Part II) covered men in certain jobs that suffered from short periods of unemployment.
- The Act only covered the worker and once the entitlement was used up the Poor Law had to be used.
- Opposition to the Insurance Act continued for some time in parts of the country.

QUESTION PRACTICE

Intermediate 1

1 Use Source 13.1 and your own knowledge to describe how Labour Exchanges helped the unemployed to find work.   *Outcome 1*

2 Study Source 13.4. Why were only certain trades covered by the Unemployment Insurance?   *Outcome 2*

Intermediate 2

1 How useful is Source 13.5 for the study of support for the National Insurance Act of 1911?   *Outcome 3*

You will need to look at the previous chapter as well to answer this 8-mark extended response.

2 What were the strengths and weaknesses of the 1911 National Insurance Act?   *Outcome 2*

14 THE LIBERAL REFORMS: AN ANSWER TO POVERTY?

In this chapter you will find out about:
* The limitations of the Reform Programme
* The important principles it introduced (Insurance, 'contribution', Pensions funded from direct taxation, etc)
* The different views of historians

The historian Edward Royle has commented that the Liberal Reforms:

SOURCE 14.1

showed a more humane understanding of poverty and sought to remove the respectable and deserving poor from the gambit of the Poor Law.

This is certainly true as the Liberal Reforms sought to provide help for people in a way that did not bring shame to the poor. This was very different from the old Poor Law. Yet the Liberal Reform programme had many limitations.
* Local authorities did not HAVE to provide school meals.
* Medical inspections for children identified a problem. It didn't cure it.
* Old Age Pensions were limited to the over 70s.
* Health Insurance only covered the worker NOT their family.
* Labour Exchanges were voluntary NOT compulsory.
* Unemployment benefit was for a very limited number of industries.

Indeed some reforms were resented by many of the people they were intended to help. The National Insurance Act in particular led to opposition. As one recent historian puts it:

SOURCE 14.2

Liberalism got relatively little political credit from the workers, who resented the compulsory contributions involved.

Yet the reforms also introduced important principles.
* The state became involved in the regulation of life for the young.
* Old Age Pensions were financed from general taxation.
* The Insurance Principle was introduced to help fund some of the social reforms.
* Pensions were administered by the Post Office removing the shame of the Poor Law.
* Unemployment benefits were administered by the Labour Exchanges not the Poor Law.

Historians disagree about the reforms and what they were trying to do. One view is that the Liberal Reforms were the starting point for

"OLIVER ASKS FOR" LESS

John Bull (fed up). "PLEASE, SIR, NEED I HAVE QUITE SO MANY GOOD THINGS?"
Mr. Lloyd George. "YES, YOU MUST. AND THERE'S MORE TO COME."

SOURCE 14.3

Some people thought Britain had had enough social reform.

reforms in the future. In particular, the Labour Reforms after the Second World War.

SOURCE 14.4

From C Cross, *The Liberals in Power.*
Two men, for politicians young men, David Lloyd George and Winston Churchill, were responsible both for reviving the Liberal Government from the doldrums of 1908 and for launching a great social programme which laid the foundations of the future Welfare State.

SOURCE 14.5

From G Williams, *The Coming of the Welfare State.*
The period from 1906 to the beginning of the First World War was one of great activity in the field of social legislation. In fact, it would be true to say that most of the developments that we now think of as part of the Welfare State are built on the foundations laid during this exciting time.

The second view is that the Liberal Reforms were very limited in their aims so we should not claim that they laid the foundations for the future 'Welfare State'.

SOURCE 14.6

From E J Evans, *Social Policy.*
We should beware of . . . claims that the Liberal Party created the Welfare State between 1906 and 1914.

SOURCE 14.7

From J R Hay, *The Origins of the Liberal Welfare Reforms.*
There were many participants in the creation of the Liberal reforms who had no thought of creating a 'welfare state' of the type which developed in Britain after 1945. Indeed many of the Liberals of 1906–14 would have been appalled by that prospect.

Other historians have tried to steer a middle way between these two views:

SOURCE 14.8

From D Fraser, *The Evolution of the British Welfare State.*
One cannot escape the conclusion that Liberal social policy before the First World War was at once at variance with the past and an anticipation of radical changes in the future.

Some in the Liberal Government of 1906–14 clearly wanted to continue reforming. As early as 1908 Winston Churchill was proposing a wide-ranging series of reforms that included:

1 Labour Exchanges and Unemployment Insurance
2 National Infirmity Insurance etc

Chapter summary

- The Liberal Reforms saw a new relationship between the Government and how it treated the poor.
- The Liberal Reforms had both strengths and weaknesses in the amount of help that was given to the poor.
- Historians disagree about the significance of the reforms.
- Some Liberals were planning further reforms before war broke out in 1914.

3 Special Expansive state Industries – Afforestation – Roads
4 Modernised Poor Law
5 Railway Amalgamation with State Control and guarantee
6 Education compulsory till the age of 17.

If it had not been for the outbreak of war in 1914, more reform seems to have been planned.

QUESTION PRACTICE

Intermediate 1

1 In what ways do historians disagree aout the importance of the Liberal Reforms? *Outcome 1*

Intermediate 2

1 Compare Sources 14.4 and 14.6 as evidence of different views of the Liberal Reforms. *Outcome 3*

2 (8-mark question)

This task is a revision exercise. You will use a lot of the information you have gathered from chapters 9, 10, 12 and 13 in your answer. Try to write an answer of at least one A4 page.

How far did the Liberal Reforms of 1906–14 deal with the problem of poverty?

You will need to look at the Liberal Reforms and judge how effective they were in dealing with poverty. What were their strengths and weaknesses? Can you come to a conclusion on each set of reforms once you have looked at this?

The following list should remind you of the main reforms.

1906   *Education (Provision of Meals) Act*: Local councils allowed to provide meals and help pay for them from rates.

1907   *Education Act*: Medical inspection of all children.

1908   *Children Act*: Known as the Children's Charter. New rules to protect children.

1908   *Labour Exchange Act.*

1908   Old Age Pensions.

1911   *National Insurance Act*: Health and Unemployment provisions.

Look at the advice about writing 8-mark answers at the end of this book.

THE FIRST WORLD WAR AND INTER-WAR YEARS

WHAT PROGRESS WAS MADE DURING THE FIRST WORLD WAR?

The First World War again identified the need to improve the physical fitness of the nation. When conscription for the army was introduced in 1916, it was found that out of every nine recruits, only three were fully fit to fight.

The size of the war forced the Government to take greater control of the country. DORA (The Defence Of The Realm Act) 1914 gave the Government wide powers. New ministries were set up to cope with wartime problems. By 1918, Ministry of Food rationed basic foods, such as tea and butter, so that everyone got a fair deal. Taxes were put up and important industries such as coal and the railways were taken under Government control.

By the end of the war, the Government had plans to carry out important welfare reforms.

SOURCE 15.1

Out of justice to the living and out of reverence to the dead, we are called to rebuild the national life on a better and more enduring foundation.

WHY DID POST-WAR WELFARE PLANS FAIL?

SOURCE 15.2

Ex-soldier protesting at the failure of the Government to deliver its promises of jobs.

Lloyd George fought the election campaign of 1918 promising a 'land fit for heroes', but big changes did not happen for several reasons:

◆ The 1918 election produced a joint Government between the Liberals and the Conservatives so Lloyd George (Liberal) was not free to do what he really wanted.

◆ The First World War caused damage to Britain's economy and so caused unemployment.

◆ From 1920 onwards, Britain's economy had a depression. Britain was too reliant on industries such as shipbuilding and coal, which had not modernised and had a lot of foreign competition. Not enough jobs were being created in new industries such as chemicals and car building.

◆ The Government had only one answer to help a poor economy: keep taxes and Government spending down. It was hoped that this would help trade recover but obviously limited the money available for social reforms.

◆ There were five different Governments between 1918 and 1929. This meant that there was no time to put plans into practice.

WHAT WERE THE EFFECTS OF THE ECONOMIC SLUMP AFTER 1929?

From 1929, a trade slump that started in the USA spread across the world. The crisis hit Europe in 1931. This caused high unemployment in Britain, which led to an increase in poverty.

In 1929, a Labour Government had been elected. Ramsay MacDonald (Prime Minister) appointed a committee to be headed by Sir George May to come up with a plan to deal with the crisis. He said that the Government had to cut spending and suggested cutting the wages of people who worked for the Government. He also said that there should be a cut in unemployment benefit. Many people in the Labour Party could not accept this and resigned from the Government. Ramsay MacDonald led a small group of people who formed a joint 'National Government' with the Conservatives and some Liberals. MacDonald and others were expelled from the Labour Party who saw them as traitors to ordinary people. Unemployment benefits were reduced by 10%. After 26 weeks, more money was only paid out after a 'means test'. The cuts were eventually restored in 1934.

FACTFILE

The Means Test
The local authority carried out an investigation into everything a family owned or earned. Even the Old Age Pension of a grandparent or a small amount earned by a child was considered. Any income coming into the household cut the amount of benefit paid. It was a humiliating experience and forced families to move apart so that they could keep the money from the Government. Ordinary people hated the means test.

SOURCE 15.3

The Scottish contingent of the 1934 Hunger march.

WHAT WERE THE LESSONS OF THE 1931 CRISIS?

- In 1932, a Royal Commission was set up to investigate unemployment benefit. It recommended that a proper national system be set up to administer state help. There were to be two national boards. One to pay out money to those who had paid National Insurance Contributions and one to take care of those who had not. These recommendations were put into practice with the 1934 Unemployment Act.

- The Government began to realise that it was not enough to react to problems of unemployment when they happened. They would have to take measures to try to cure unemployment. Government Training Centres for the Unemployed were set up. Areas of high unemployment were given 'special area' status. It was hoped this would encourage investment. These measures were well meaning but the centres did not guarantee jobs and the 'special areas' were not very successful at attracting new firms.

TIMELINE – KEY CHANGES IN WELFARE

Reform	Progress Made
1918 Fisher Education Act	Fees for primary schools were abolished. The school leaving age was raised to 14.
1919 Ministry of Health	State supervision of health, the poor and insurance schemes. Also housing, until 1921 the Government gave money to encourage council house building.
1920 Insurance Act	Unemployment benefits extended to all workers earning up to £5 a week except in farming, civil service and domestic service.
1924 Housing Act	A Labour scheme to assist council house building. £9 per house for 40 years was offered to councils. The rent for these houses was still too dear for many working people.
1925 Old Age Pensions Act	This gave pensions to people over the age of 65 who had made enough National Insurance Contributions. (Normal pension age – 70)
1934 Unemployment Act	The Unemployment Assistance Board was set up to see that the out of work were paid the same across the country. State and not local funding to be used.

WHAT PROGRESS HAD BEEN MADE BY 1939?

- By 1939 there were signs that the Government was beginning to realise that it was not enough to react to crises, it had to try to prevent problems. Even if, as with unemployment, the measures taken were of limited success.
- There was a renewed growth in caring voluntary charities and societies. They worked in partnership with the Government under the National Council for Social Services.
- The areas in which people could get help was also extended. Social services now included housing and education was well as poverty and health.
- There was growing awareness of the social neglect and division in British society. Writers such as J B Priestley, who had done a tour of Britain in 1934, helped influence the desire for more community action.

Chapter summary
- First World War increased Government powers.
- Expectations of big post-war changes failed to happen owing to economic and political crises.
- Increased Government responsibility for social services.
- More pressure for state action to solve social problems.

16

THE EFFECTS OF THE SECOND WORLD WAR: THE EXPERIENCE OF WAR

In this chapter you will find out about:
◆ The effects of war on the Home Front and Government
◆ The effects of evacuation and German bombing
◆ Rationing and its effects

WHAT WAS THE EFFECT OF WAR ON THE HOME FRONT?

The Second World War broke out in 1939 but serious fighting did not start until 1940. It was clear that the war was not going to be short. After the retreat of the British Army from Dunkirk, a new national mood developed and people were determined to beat Hitler and create a better Britain.

This chapter is about how the Second World War united communities and brought together people who in peacetime had little to do with each other. Many people found out about social problems for the first time. This and people's suffering in the war led to the determination to create a better world once the war was over.

THE GOVERNMENT

Soon after the start of the war, Winston Churchill replaced Neville Chamberlain as Prime Minister. He created a Government that included all the main political parties. This was called the Coalition Government. By including everyone, Churchill hoped to show Britain's determination to defeat Hitler.

Several members of the Labour Party were given important jobs as Government ministers. Clement Attlee became the Deputy Prime Minister. Ernest Bevin, leader of the Transport and General Workers' Union, was given the job of Minister of Labour. This was a key job in organising the war effort at home. Posts were also given to Arthur Greenwood, Herbert Morrison and Stafford Cripps. Labour was the party that had made further welfare reform an important part of their policies. Now they had a chance to get experience of Government and making decisions.

SOURCE 16.1

From M Shinwell, *The Labour Story.*
After the initial shock of Nazi successes there developed a sense of having an almost impossible job to do – and to achieve success ... when a meeting of the Joint Executive took place, there was virtually unanimous agreement that Labour should serve under Churchill.

A Coalition Government
A coalition government is one made up of more than one political party. The Coalition Government was set up in May 1940 and lasted until 1945. It was led by Winston Churchill and included representatives from the Conservative, Labour and Liberal parties.

EVACUATION

SOURCE 16.2

Evacuees queuing for buses in Glasgow Road, Clydebank, 1941.

For years people had lived with the fear that if there were a war, 'the bomber would always get through'. German planes had the ability to destroy important factories, communications and military targets. The Government worried that German bombing would kill too many people and so organised the moving of children away from areas likely to be attacked. The condition of some of the children from deprived areas came as a shock to middle-class country dwellers. On the other hand, some of the evacuees did not like the treatment they got at the places they went to.

SOURCE 16.3

Resulting from the Government's evacuation of children, the City and County of Perth received many thousands of mothers, children of school age and pre-school children from Glasgow. From practically all districts complaints have been received concerning the verminous and filthy condition of the children.
Perthshire Advertiser, 20 September 1939

SOURCE 16.4

The group of kids had been so neglected that they just stripped the clothes off them and had a great, hot bath ready. But this wee lad wasn't going to go into that bath and he screamed and yelled some incoherent phrase over and over again, and spread his arms and legs so they couldn't get him into the bath. Lady Elgin asked the housekeeper 'What is he saying?' The housekeeper replied, 'He's saying it's ower effin' deep and its ower effin' hot.'

Most of the evacuation took place at the beginning of the war. There were two main effects of evacuation:

1 Different sections of society met up and socialised with each other in a way unheard of in peacetime.
2 It raised awareness of continuing social problems, which many assumed to have disappeared.

Both of these helped to unite Britain and give its people a common experience and purpose.

THE BOMBING

Soon after the start of war, the Germans started to bomb key factories, transport and communication links. As well as London, most of the big industrial towns were targeted – Manchester, Liverpool and Coventry all suffered heavy damage. In Scotland, Glasgow, Dundee and Edinburgh were targeted. Aberdeen was the most bombed city in Scotland with 34 attacks. Most of these were 'tip and run' raids – bombers who had missed their targets dropping their bombs before going home.

Very often the bombers missed their targets resulting in damage to civilian areas. The bombing destroyed the homes of rich and poor alike. Again, it brought together people who normally had little to do with each other. The bombings helped to develop community spirit and helped lead to further welfare reforms.

SOURCE 16.5

A bombed tenement building in Clydeside in which 80 people died..

SOURCE 16.6

Cartoon by David Low showing Goering's Luftwaffe bombing the East End of London. The caption says 'Impregnable target'.

SOURCE 16.7

From R M Titmuss, *Problems of Social Policy*.

... Damage to homes and injuries to persons were not less likely among the rich than the poor so ... the assistance provided by the government ... was offered to all groups in the community. The pooling of national resources and the sharing of risks ... were the guiding principles. Acceptance of these principles moved forward the goals of welfare. New obligations were shouldered, higher standards were set.

RATIONING AND ITS EFFECTS

In peacetime, Britain depended on imports – 60% of its food came from abroad. As soon as the Nazis gained control of most of Europe, food supplies dropped. The shortages caused queuing and rising prices. This was unfair as the rich could afford to pay prices the poor couldn't. To ensure 'fair shares for all', the Government introduced food rationing in 1940 and clothes rationing in 1941. Coupons as well as money were needed to buy goods in short supply.

SOURCE 16.8

From the diary of Miss C M Edwards, Birbrook, Lincolnshire, 28 September 1943

I think the food authorities have done a wonderful job. There's really no shortage anywhere of essentials.

Rationing helped establish the idea of universal and equal share of the 'national cake'. In people's minds, it was unacceptable for some to be better off when everyone was fighting the war. It also led to the Government taking more direct control of the nation's health. As in the First World War, the Government was forced to interfere more in people's daily lives.

SOURCE 16.9

From J Davis, *The Wartime Kitchen Garden: The Home Front 1939–1945*.
Rationing was achieving its aim of distribution that enables everyone to get their fair share. In fact shoppers wanted more articles put on ration.

> **Chapter summary**
> ◆ Second World War united the different communities and classes of Britain with a common aim.
> ◆ A national Government was formed to represent the nation's unity.
> ◆ Bombing, evacuation and rationing raised awareness of continuing social problems.
> ◆ The suffering of the war caused a determination to deal with welfare problems once the war was over – to create a better society.

QUESTION PRACTICE

Intermediate 1

Source A

From H Jackson, *Scotland's War*.
*When they came we were full of good will. And we thought,
'Oh the poor dears coming from the towns will be so pleased
to come to this beautiful country place' ... But one lady was
very irate at being given children who were obviously
verminous [had head lice]'*

1 Describe how country people reacted to evacuees.

Outcome 1

Source B

From J Beavan in, *The People's War* by Peter Lewis.
*Peace-time society always tends to be a battle for oneself – a
me first situation. In the war this was blessedly different.
Everybody felt they should do what they could for someone else
if they were bombed out, the nearest families took them in.*

2 In what ways did the war change how people behaved?

Outcome 2

Intermediate 2

Source C

From D Healey *in The People's War* by Peter Lewis.
*The big thing about the war was that it mixed people up, it
broke down the class and occupational barriers that existed
before. Everybody had a value and in that sense all men and
all women were equal. This had a profound effect on people's
attitude to social and economic problems.*

1 Explain how the Second World War changed people's
attitudes towards social problems. *Outcome 2*

17 THE IMPACT OF THE SECOND WORLD WAR: CHANGING GOVERNMENT

HOW DID GOVERNMENT CONTROL OVER PEOPLE'S LIVES INCREASE?

Unlike the First World War, the Home Front during the Second World War was treated and run like a battlefield. The daily threat of bombing combined with shortages of both supplies and workers meant that everyone had to have their lives controlled by the Government. The priority was to ensure 'fair shares for all' and to avoid waste. For example, the designs of many goods and clothing were standardised.

CONSCRIPTION

Conscription was introduced for young men in the armed services. People could also find themselves conscripted to work in essential industries such as coal-mining and farming. The biggest change in the workplace was probably experienced by women. Britain was the only country during the Second World War to conscript women for the war effort. Unmarried women could be called up to the armed forces and other women directed to work elsewhere. They replaced men in jobs that were considered to be traditionally male and played a vital part in ensuring that food production was maintained.

SOURCE 17.1

Women working on the railways in Glasgow, around 1942.

During the Second World War there was also a change in the Government's attitude to managing the economy. The cost of the fighting forced the Government to abandon its pre-war principle of minimum tax and spending. Taxes were increased and Britain became heavily reliant on the 'Lend-Lease' loans from America. One of Churchill's expert advisers was the economist J. M. Keynes. He believed that it was the Government's responsibility to ensure that Britain's economy would be successful. In particular, he believed that a successful economy should provide full employment for its people. The only way to do that was by state action and public spending. His ideas were influential during the Second World War and after.

THE MINISTRY OF FOOD

In April 1940, Lord Woolton became the Minister of Food. He realised that if everyone was to get a balanced diet then the Government would have to control food production and supplies. The Ministry of Food's job was not just about ensuring everyone got a fair share of the food. It also aimed to improve the nation's health in order to improve the ability to fight. To this end, the Ministry of Food planned the rationing scheme so that calcium, iron, minerals and vitamins were added to certain foods.

SOURCE 17.2

Advert promoting free vitamins and cod liver oil to children.

Throughout the war, the Ministry of Food organised an advice and propaganda campaign. They published a series of 'Food Facts' leaflets giving nutritional information plus recipes. Lord Woolton also got a comedy music hall duo 'Gert' and 'Daisy' to go round the country promoting the food economy message. In April 1940, the National Food Education Campaign was launched. This involved nation-wide cookery demonstrations to help women make the most of home-produced foods.

SOURCE 17.3

A cookery demonstration in a London store.

Just as in the previous war, the Second World War showed up the underlying social problems in British society. It was recognised that there was a need for a general system of help, for poorer people, organised and paid for by the state.

In 1942, a plan was published that at last seemed to answer that need. It was called the Beveridge Report, and offered an overall plan for the British system of welfare.

WHY WAS THE MINISTRY OF FOOD IMPORTANT?

- The Ministry of Food is important as evidence of the extent of Government control during the Second World War.
- Its activities established the principle of Government responsibility for promoting the nation's health and ensuring a safe food supply.
- The Ministry of Food was the first nationwide attempt to apply nutrition knowledge in the world. It had such a reputation for having done a good job that after the war it attracted visiting nutritionists from other countries.
- The work of the Ministry continued after the Second World War. Food rationing for products such as meat lasted until 1953 and bread rationing did not start until 1946 owing to the shortage of cereals. Advice on nutrition has continued to the present day.

SOURCE 17.4

Free school meals.

WELFARE REFORM DURING THE WAR

TIMELINE – KEY CHANGES IN WELFARE

Reform	Progress Made
1941 Emergency Milk and Meals Scheme	Extra rations were given to expectant mothers and young children. Cheap cod liver oil, milk and orange juice were given to mothers. The price of milk and school meals was subsidised by the Government. Free food was given to children who needed it.
Health Care	War wounded (including bomb victims) were given free treatment. 'Emergency beds' were also provided that were paid for by the state. Free immunisation programme against diptheria greatly decreased the number of deaths.
1941 Supplementary Payments Scheme	Extra help was given to Old Age Pensioners who found it hard to manage.
1941 Abolition of Means Test	The hated inquiry into all the earnings of an unemployed man's family was done away with.
1945 Family Allowances Scheme	Extra money to be paid to families with two children or more.

SOURCE 17.5

From H Glennerster in David Gladstone, *The Twentieth Century Welfare State.*

Almost all the ideas and proposals for reform in social security and education, for example, had been discussed in the 1920s and 1930s.

TO WHAT EXTENT DID THE SECOND WORLD WAR CAUSE THE WELFARE STATE?

From the information above it is easy to see the main effects of the Second World War:
- The suffering made people determined to create a better society after the war.
- The Government took a much greater role in helping people.
- The British public expected their Government to do more for them.
- Pressure to plan to rebuild Britain after the war had led to Churchill's Government drawing up plans to tackle some of Beveridge's 'five giants' (see Chapter 18).

But historians have disagreed about how important the Second World War was in causing welfare reform:

SOURCE 17.6

From J MacNicol in D Gladstone, *The Twentieth Century Welfare State*.
... the sheer scale and magnitude of the events that took place during those six crucial years seems to lend indisputable credibility to the view that modern wars are a major force behind progressive social change.

Chapter summary
- War caused the Government to get more involved in all areas of people's lives.
- The Ministry of Food established the responsibility of the Government to ensure the nation's health and a safe food supply.
- War highlighted the underlying problems in British society and the need for centrally organised, overall welfare policy.
- Historians disagree about how important the Second World War was in causing the Welfare State.

QUESTION PRACTICE

Intermediate 1

1 Look at Source 17.4. What help was given to children by the Government during the Second World War?
Outcome 1

Source A is from the diary of Miss C. M. Edwards, dated 28 September, 1943:

But seriously, I think the food authorities have done a wonderful job. There's really no shortage anywhere of essentials.

2 How accurate is Source A in showing how people reacted to Government rationing?
Outcome 3

Intermediate 2

1 To what extent do Sources 17.5 and 17.6 disagree about the Second World War causing the Welfare State?
Outcome 3

2 Explain how the Second World War changed people's attitudes to government intervention.
(8-mark extended response)
Outcome 2

18 THE BEVERIDGE REPORT AND THE 'FIVE GIANTS' OF POVERTY

In this chapter you will find out about:
- Who Beveridge was
- The Five Giants of Want, Disease, Ignorance, Squalor and Idleness
- Main points of the Beveridge Report
- Why The Beveridge Report was important
- Progress before 1945
- The 1944 Butler Education Act

WHO WAS BEVERIDGE?

Beveridge (1879–1963) was born in India and was educated at the private school Charterhouse and at Oxford University. He became an expert on social welfare and unemployment problems and helped Churchill and Lloyd George with the writing of the laws for the Labour Exchanges and insurance during the time of the Liberal Government, 1906–1914. His best known work was done as chairman of the committee that produced the 'Report on Social Insurance and Allied Services' in 1942. Beveridge used this report to set out his vision of welfare support 'from the cradle to the grave'. Its aims went much further than Churchill wanted but they immediately became popular with the British public and the report became a best seller. The report helped shape the social policy of both the Coalition Government from 1944–1945 and the Labour Government after 1945.

WHAT WERE THE 'FIVE GIANTS' OF WANT, DISEASE, IGNORANCE, SQUALOR AND IDLENESS?

The five giants were the problems that Beveridge believed stood in the way of social progress. Beveridge had been asked to look at the question of providing a proper system of sickness and unemployment benefit to workers when needed. However, Beveridge argued that such benefits were only part of the answer to achieving social progress.

SOURCE 18.2

Beveridge said:

Social insurance may provide income security, it is an attack on Want. But Want is one of only five giants. The others are Disease, Ignorance, Squalor, and Idleness.

In order to fight these giants it would be necessary to also provide a proper national health service and family allowances to those with children. Most importantly, the Government should undertake a policy of full employment.

Beveridge believed that tackling just one of the five giants wouldn't do much good. If the welfare of the British people were to improve, then the Government would have to try and solve all the

TRANSFORMATION SCENE
"Avaunt, foul spirte! and be no longer seen
I'll have you know I am the Fairy Queen!"

SOURCE 18.1

Cartoon from Punch showing Beveridge as the 'good fairy' banishing the 'demon' Want.

problems that stood in its way. His ideas provided the basis for the policies of the 'Welfare State'.

WHAT WERE THE MAIN POINTS OF THE BEVERIDGE REPORT?

Below is a summary of the Report's main recommendations:
- A Government Minister to be appointed to control all the benefits schemes.
- A national health service should be set up.
- Standard weekly National Insurance Contributions to be made by people in work.
- Unemployed people to have the right to payments for an indefinite period.
- Payments to be made at a standard rate, without a means test.
- Benefits to include Old Age Pensions, maternity grants, pensions for widows and people injured at work.
- Family allowances to be introduced.

REACTION TO THE BEVERIDGE REPORT

The report was enthusiastically received – and not just by the public. In Parliament, 97 Labour and 22 Liberal and Conservatives voted for the Report to be put into operation as soon as possible.

SOURCE 18.3

Beveridge said:

The scheme proposed here is in some ways a revolution but in more important ways it is a natural development from the past. It is a British revolution.

SOURCE 18.4

Press Reaction:
The Daily Telegraph's *front page, 2 December 1942.*

SOURCE 18.5

From S Robertson and L Wilson, *Scotland's War*.
I was in a prisoner-of-war camp when the Beveridge report came out. Somebody had a copy sent to them and the excitement that this caused was quite marked, and there were big discussions and debates about why we had been fighting.

SOURCE 18.6

From Brooke in *The Twentieth Century Welfare State* by David Gladstone.
the Beveridge Report ... became an icon for the labour movement.

SOURCE 18.7

From D Gladstone, *The Twentieth Century Welfare State*.
... the Conservatives were more lukewarm and divided in their response.

CRITICISMS OF BEVERIDGE

Not everyone was delighted with the Beveridge Report. Some people did not want the Government's interference in their homes and others worried about the cost:

SOURCE 18.8

... we did not start this war with Germany in order to improve our social services; the war was forced upon us by Germany and we entered into it to preserve our freedom and to keep the Gestapo outside our houses, and that is what the war means.
Sir John Forbes Watson, Director of the Confederation of British Employers

SOURCE 18.9

The broad impression left by the report on the ordinary reader is that ... the general finance of the scheme can be carried out without any undue difficulty. There are, however ... doubts and uncertainties suggesting that large financial commitments cannot be undertaken without misgivings.
Sir Kingsley Wood, 1942

Other people were critical of the fact that contributions alone would not pay for the scheme – extra funding would have to come from general taxation. Also, that the needs of married women, disabled and single parent families were not fully catered for. However, one historian thinks we ought to give Beveridge the credit for achieving such a groundbreaking report:

SOURCE 18.10

From 'Founders of the Welfare State' by Paul Barker
Perhaps it is time that we stopped blaming Beveridge for our own failures and gave him the recognition he deserves for transforming the rickety structure of pre-war social security into a building whose structures have proved remarkably solid.

WHY WAS THE BEVERIDGE REPORT IMPORTANT?

The Beveridge Report was important for four main reasons:

1 It simplified existing insurance benefits and generalised the level of payments.
2 It had revolutionary ideas. Firstly, that society could, and should fight the five giants of poverty. Secondly, that people not only had freedom *to* do things, but the freedom *from* certain things like want, disease etc. Third, that the scheme should be **universal**, that is, applied to everyone.
3 It established the principle that people were **entitled** to benefits as they had made insurance contributions when working. This took away the stigma of getting state help.
4 The scheme proposed was the same for everyone. All working people would pay the same into the scheme and get the same benefits. This meant that everyone got a fair deal.

WHAT PROGRESS WAS MADE TOWARDS THE BEVERIDGE REPORT BEFORE 1945?

The Labour Party is generally credited with putting the Beveridge Report into action, but the Coalition Government did at least make a start.

◆ In 1943, a ministry to supervise insurance benefits was set up.
◆ In 1945, the Family Allowance was passed. However, the level of benefits was not as generous as Beveridge had wanted – and payments were delayed for a year.
◆ The Ministry of Town and County Planning was set up in 1943 and immediately produced proposals for new towns to ease congestion around London. Temporary housing was built for the homeless and the price of building materials controlled to stop the price of houses rising out of control.

The Government also published a number of White Papers (proposals for future action) on the national health service, employment policy and social insurance. All of these showed that the Coalition Government accepted much of the Beveridge Report. For the most part however, action taken by the Coalition Government was not especially radical. Churchill wanted to concentrate on winning the war, and the peace, before turning his attention to domestic matters. The exception was the area of education.

THE BUTLER EDUCATION ACT 1944

SOURCE 18.11

RAB Butler, Conservative MP, Minister of Education.

Evacuation had shown the need for universal improvement in education. Education was thought to be an important way of fighting poverty. It made for an educated workforce who could expect better paid jobs.

◆ The Education Act created the post of Minister for Education and a comprehensive education system.

◆ For the first time, three stages of educational development were defined: Primary, Secondary and Further. All education authorities had to provide these stages.

◆ Fees for local authority schools were abolished (although not at direct-grant grammar schools) so there was free education for all up to school leaving age. This was set at 15 from 1945.

The reforms were well received at the time:

SOURCE 18.12

Cartoon by David Low showing Butler using 'education cement' to help rebuild democracy. The caption says: 'I know what it needs, boss! Foundations!

CRITICISMS OF EDUCATION REFORM

The Education Act has been criticised for setting up divisions in the education system.

- By allowing selective grammar schools to continue to exist, a two-tier system was created which resulted in the whole adult future of a teenager being decided by the type of school they went to when they were 11 or 12.
- A grammar school pupil could expect to go on to university and then to a professional job.
- A secondary modern school pupil would do practical subjects and then do a skilled or semi-skilled trade.
- Critics have argued that young people from poorer backgrounds were discriminated against because they were more likely to go to a secondary modern school and so have their future choices limited.

However, some historians have pointed out that it was not the Act itself that caused the divisions:

SOURCE 18.13

From D Fraser, *The Evolution of the Welfare State.*
The 1944 Act did not in fact legislate for the divisions within secondary education that caused so much later controversy. These lay in the logic of the Hadow and Spens Reports and had been confirmed by the Norwood Committee in 1943 which found three sorts of pupils which neatly fitted in with the three sorts of schools available, grammar, technical and modern.

The Labour Government has been criticised for not adding anything new to the wartime Coalition Government's policy:

SOURCE 18.14

From Kenneth Morgan.
It is hard to avoid the view that education was an area where the Labour Government failed to provide new ideas or inspiration, although the new investment, the new impetus at elementary level, and the large increase in the school population did pave the way for the educational boom of the fifties and sixties.

Chapter summary
In this chapter you will have learned about:
- The importance of William Beveridge.
- The main points of the Beveridge Report and its importance.
- Progress made towards the Beveridge Report by 1945.
- The 1944 Education Act and some criticisms of it.

QUESTION PRACTICE

Intermediate 1
Source A

Interest in The Beveridge Plan on its publication was really tremendous ... one report says. There has been possibly more widespread discussion on this than on any single event since the outbreak of war.
Ministry of Information document, 18 March 1943

1 How accurate is Source A as evidence of public reaction to the Beveridge Report?   *Outcome 3*

 Source B is from The Beveridge Report.

Social insurance should be treated as one part only of a comprehensive policy of social progress. Social insurance fully developed may provide income security; it is an attack upon Want. But want is only one of the five giants on the road of reconstruction and in some way the easiest to attack. The others are Disease, Ignorance, Squalor and Idleness.

2 What social problems did the Beveridge Report aim to solve?   *Outcome 1*

Intermediate 2
Source C

A dangerous optimism is growing up about the conditions it will be possible to establish here after the war ... While not disheartening our people by dwelling on the dark side of things, Ministers should, in my view, be careful not to raise false hopes, as was done the last time by speeches about 'homes fit for heroes.
Winston Churchill in a Cabinet note, 12 January, 1943.

1 Describe Churchill's attitude to the Beveridge Report.   *Outcome 1*

2 Study Source 18.8. Why did some people oppose the Beveridge Report?   *Outcome 2*

19

THE ELECTION OF 1945 – A WELFARE STATE?

In this chapter you will find out about:
- The campaigns
- Why Labour won (social reforms, industrial reforms and foreign policy)
- The idea of the Welfare State
- Paying for reform (incl. American loans)

THE CAMPAIGNS FOR THE 1945 ELECTION

POPULAR OPINION

The mood of the people once the war was over was clear. They wanted a reward for all their suffering and hardships. There was a real worry that the promises of homes, jobs and social security would be empty promises – just like after the First World War:

SOURCE 19.1

Cartoon from the Daily Mirror, June 1945.

SOURCE 19.2

Cartoon by David Low showing a group of rich businessmen raising the same objections to social reform in 1919 and 1943. In the cartoon the businessmen are saying 'Too risky. Too expensive, Against our traditions, Against our interests' and the caption says 'What Again?'

THE CONSERVATIVE AND LABOUR ELECTION CAMPAIGNS

SOURCE 19.3

Winston Churchill in an election broadcast, 4 June 1945.

I declare to you ... that no Socialist system can be established without a political police ... No Socialist Government conducting the entire life and industry of the country could afford to allow free, sharp, or violently-worded expressions of public discontent. They would have to fall back on some form of Gestapo, no doubt very humanely directed in the first instance.

THE ELECTION RESULT

The policies of the two main parties were not very different, especially in the area of social reform. After all, the planning and some reforms for the Welfare State had already been passed before 1945. However, it seemed that the electorate trusted the promises of the Labour Party more, and elected them with 393 seats compared to the Conservative's 213.

It may seem surprising that people did not fully trust Churchill and the Conservatives. He had been an outstanding war leader, who had kept the nation going through some very hard times.

WHY DID LABOUR WIN THE ELECTION?

There were several reasons for Labour's popularity:
- People remembered the grand promises made by the Liberals and Conservatives after the First World War – and that they had not been delivered.
- Labour had consistently supported social reform in the inter-war period whereas the Conservatives had been the party who had supported cuts in spending during the Depression.
- The Beveridge Report had been massively popular but it had been noticed that Churchill was not as enthusiastic. He was worried that Britain would not be able to afford large-scale social help. This sounded too much like the attitudes of governments who had failed to bring in reforms after the First World War.
- Churchill had alienated some people with his personal attacks on Attlee. He had campaigned on a ticket of 'winning the peace'. This would mean heavy spending on defence – and attention spent on foreign affairs. People wanted money to be spent on domestic needs rather than weapons. A war-weary British population wanted life to get back to normal.
- During the hard times of the war, the idea of a Welfare State had given many people a dream worth fighting for. People voted for the Party they believed most likely to deliver their dream.

SOURCE 19.4

Clement Attlee and his wife celebrate the Labour landslide victory.

SOURCE 19.5

From D Howell, British Social Democracy, in *Hindsight*, 1999.
Bread, butter plus a dream. That was the secret of 1945.

SOURCE 19.6

From K Morgan, Labour in Power 1945–51, *Hindsight*, 1998.
Labour was uniquely identified with a sweeping change of mood during the war years. Labour alone seemed to understand and project the new mood.

SOURCE 19.7

Cartoon by David Low showing the belief that Churchill's policy aims contradicted each other.

SOURCE 19.8

From *A People's War*.
... the election, in which the party programmes ... had much in common, turned on the question of credibility. Which of them was most likely to fulfil the general promises of wide-ranging social reforms? Ever since Churchill turned down Beveridge there was only one answer.

WHAT WAS THE WELFARE STATE?

FACTFILE

The Welfare State was a system of state help and benefits. It was started in 1945 by the Labour Government and aimed to do away with the causes of poverty. These had been identified in 1942 by William Beveridge as Want, Disease, Ignorance, Squalor and Idleness.

The Welfare State was different from government help that had existed before for three main reasons:

1 It was a universal scheme that applied to everyone.
2 Benefits were centrally organised and given out by the Government.
3 People were now entitled to benefits having paid flat rate National Insurance Contributions from their pay packets.

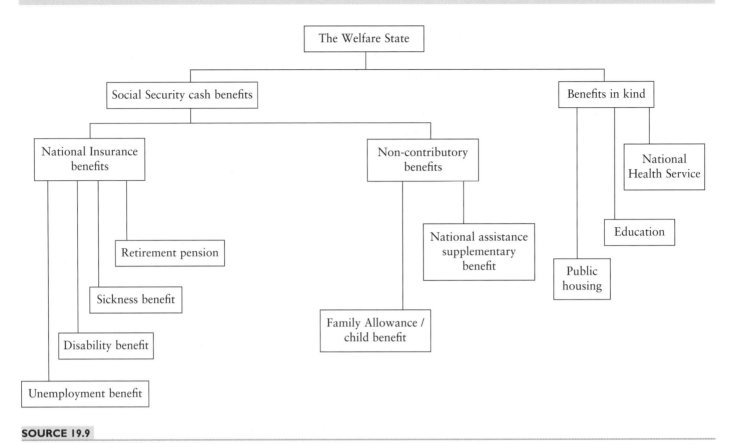

SOURCE 19.9

A definition of the benefits of a Welfare State.

HOW DID THE GOVERNMENT PAY FOR THE REFORMS?

By 1948, the Labour Government had set up most of the services that made up the Welfare State. It was a remarkable achievement given the death and destruction caused to Britain by the Second World War: the economy and essential industries were badly run down. Britain had been forced to sell £1,000 million of foreign investments and exports had been deeply cut, as had the number of merchant ships.

Britain also owed a great deal of money to America. She had fought the war with goods and materials from America under a 'Lend-Lease' agreement. Britain was supposed to pay for these at some point and owed America over £3,000 million. She still needed the help given by America but when the war ended, so did the aid. The problems faced by the Labour Government were made worse by a severe winter in 1947–8 and the unstable relations between the Western countries and Russia. It seemed an unwise time to disarm, but spending on the army was a drain on the Government's resources.

Some economists and civil servants thought that Britain could not afford the Welfare State and wanted to postpone it. But Clement Attlee was determined that Labour would not betray its election promises.

Chapter summary

In this chapter you will have learnt about:

◆ The election campaign of 1945.

◆ Why Labour won the election.

◆ What was the Welfare State.

◆ How the Labour Government paid for the reforms.

Money was raised in several ways:

◆ Essential industries were nationalised so that the Government could firmly control the economy. These included coal, electricity, gas, the railways and waterways, airways and the Bank of England.

◆ Rationing continued on food, fuel and clothing and the choice of consumer goods in shops was still limited.

◆ The economist J M Keynes negotiated a further loan from America. Unfortunately, Britain had to pay interest on the loan and also suffered a currency crisis as America insisted that controls on exchanging money be relaxed.

◆ Britain received about £2,400 in 'Marshall Aid'. This was money from America to help allies against the spread of Communism from Russia. They hoped to make countries like Britain well-off so as to provide a barrier around Communism.

It took a great deal of courage for the Labour Government to push ahead with the reforms in such a situation. However, even at the start of the Welfare State it was obvious that paying for it was going to be less than easy.

QUESTION PRACTICE

Intermediate 1

Source A

While he has outstandingly maintained his position as a popular war leader, his position as a post-war figure is far from certain in the public mind ... His age, his already almost complete achievement, his supposed disinterest in home affairs, and his alleged lack of sympathy with working people over domestic issues, all add up in the public mind.
A Mass Observation (Opinion Poll report about Churchill), in *The New Statesman*, 1943

1 Explain why people did not vote for Churchill in the 1945 election. *Outcome 2*

Intermediate 2

1 How far do the cartoons in Sources 19.1 and 19.2 agree on what people wanted in Britain in 1945?
Outcome 3

2 Describe the problems faced by Britain's economy after the Second World War. *Outcome 1*

20

THE LABOUR REFORMS: NATIONAL INSURANCE, NATIONAL ASSISTANCE AND NATIONALISATION

In this chapter you will find out about:
- The 1946 National Insurance Act
- Industrial Injuries Act
- 1948 National Assistance Board
- Nationalisation
- Putting the reforms into practice

THE 1946 NATIONAL INSURANCE ACT

Almost everyone welcomed the new universal insurance scheme. Both Labour and Conservatives made speeches in favour of it.

Main points of the 1946 National Insurance Act:
- Benefits were set up for unemployment, sickness, maternity and widows.
- Allowances were paid to guardians/parents in charge of children.
- Retirement pensions were paid.
- Death grant given to help with funeral expenses.
- Rates of benefit: basic rate 26 shillings a week. For a married man 42 shillings. 7s 6d extra for first child.

James Griffiths was the man who was in charge of making Beveridge's dream a reality. He went further than Beveridge had expected and gave pensions to old people at once rather than waiting for a 20 year delay. He also passed the Industrial Injuries Act.

Main points of the 1946 Industrial Injuries Act:
- Payments for those temporarily hurt.
- Long-term payments for anyone permanently unable to work. This group also got a higher rate of benefit than someone just out of a job.

In 1948, the National Assistance Board was set up to help people not covered by the National Insurance Act. Some had found that the benefits were not enough to live on in the long term. Old people, especially, found that their benefits did not keep up with the cost of living.

Main work done by the National Assistance Board:
- People had to undergo a 'needs test'.
- Provide help to needy people not covered by the National Insurance Act.
- Interview applicants claiming help to assess genuine need.

◆ Provide weekly or one-off payments for problems such as bedding or clothing.

The National Insurance and assistance schemes were a great leap forward in setting a basic standard of living for all. But they needed a great number of Government workers to be put into practice.

SOURCE 20.1

The first Family Allowance day in Stratford, East London, 6 August, 1946.

NATIONALISATION

Beveridge had insisted that full employment could solve the problem of poverty. Without it, social services would only cure the symptoms of poverty, and not the causes. The Labour Government was fully committed to the idea of full employment. It fitted in with their idea that the economy should be tightly controlled by the Government.

One of the ways in which the Government did this was to nationalise certain key industries. Government control of key industries was an important socialist principle. Nationalisation took place as follows:
◆ 1946, Bank of England, civil aviation
◆ 1947, National Coal Board, cables and wireless
◆ 1948, British Transport Commission (road, rail, etc), electricity
◆ 1949, Gas
◆ 1950, Iron and Steel.

Nationalisation was a mixed success. It kept unemployment very low, but some industries, like coal-mining, were very badly run and cost the Government money.

PUTTING THE REFORMS INTO PRACTICE

In July 1948, the whole of the Welfare State started operating. The setting up of the Welfare State created thousands of new government jobs and many government offices. There was also a big increase in the amount of information that the Government held on an individual. More than ever before, the Government had knowledge of, and could interfere in a person's 'private life'.

From the Labour Government's point of view, it mostly worked very well. In the first year of the insurance scheme there was actually a surplus as the Government saved money owing to the low level of unemployment. On the other hand, the National Health Service cost far more – and costs continued to rise. This took the Government by surprise. Although they had expected an initial demand they had not calculated on the high continued use of the scheme. Bevan said at the time:

SOURCE 20.2

I shudder to think of the ceaseless cascade of medicine which is pouring down British throats at the present time.

Aneurin Bevan

Chapter summary

In this chapter you will have learnt about:

◆ How the Labour Government put Beveridge's insurance scheme into practice.

◆ The main points of the reforms.

◆ Putting the reforms into practice.

QUESTION PRACTICE

Intermediate 1

Source A Clement Atlee said:

We now recognise that to allow, through mass unemployment or through sickness, great numbers of people to be ineffective as consumers is an economic loss to the country.

1 What were the benefits of the National Insurance Bill?

Outcome 1

Intermediate 2

Source B D Fraser, a modern historian, identified that:

Four Acts had constructed a social security network which protected everyone against destitution or want; these were the 1945 Family Allowance Act, the 1948 National Insurance Act, and Industrial Injuries Acts and the 1948 National Assistance Act.

1 Explain how people were provided with a social security network by 1948.

Outcome 2

21

THE LABOUR REFORMS: THE NATIONAL HEALTH SERVICE

In this chapter you will find out about:
- Aneurin Bevan and the building of the Health Service
- Opposition of the doctors
- Winning over opposition
- Putting the Health Service into practice
- Problems with the NHS

WHO WAS ANEURIN BEVAN?

FACTFILE

Bevan was the son of a Welsh coal-miner and he also worked down the pits from the age of 13. He soon became an active trade unionist and helped in the General Strike of 1926. From 1929, he was the Labour MP for Ebbw Vale. He was a brilliant speaker and was known for his strong Socialist views. Bevan became Minister of Health, 1945–51. He was responsible for introducing the National Health Service and trying to solve the post-war housing problems. Bevan resigned as Minister of Health when prescription charges were introduced in 1951.

BEVAN AND THE BUILDING OF THE HEALTH SERVICE

SOURCE 21.1

A person ought to be able to receive hospital and medical help without being involved in financial anxiety.
Bevan

Bevan's biggest problem in setting up the Health Service was getting the co-operation of the doctors and dentists. They were in no mood to lose their independence. They were worried that they would be turned into Government workers, sent wherever the Government wanted to put them. The Bill for the National Health Service was passed in 1946 with a two-year delay before it was put into practice. Bevan hoped to use the time to get the doctors on his side.

THE OPPOSITION OF THE DOCTORS

Many hospital workers were keen on the Health Service reforms. By the end of the Second World War, many hospitals were in need of modernising and new, expensive equipment. They saw the Health Service as being their only way of getting what they needed.

The real opposition came from the General Practitioners (GPs). In 1946, an opinion poll showed that 64% of GPs were opposed to Bevan's plans. They believed that his reforms would destroy a doctor's freedom to treat a patient as he wished. The British Medical Association organised a fierce campaign of resistance against Bevan.

HOW DID BEVAN WIN OVER THE DOCTORS?

Bevan had already won over health workers such as dentists.
◆ Bevan promised the hospital workers the buildings and equipment they needed.
◆ He also agreed that doctors could continue to treat private as well as Health Service patients.
◆ Doctors would get a salary and the right to earn more money with private patients. Each hospital would have some private beds for people who wanted to have private treatment.

This left the GPs isolated against public opinion which was strongly in favour of the new National Health Service (NHS). By 1948 Bevan had persuaded a quarter of doctors in England, and a third of doctors in Scotland and Wales, to sign up for the NHS. At this point organised opposition collapsed and the Health Service started working in July 1948.

SOURCE 21.2

Cartoon by David Low showing Bevan getting the co-operation of the dentists by shoving money into their pockets. The caption says 'Open wide, please. I'm afraid this might hurt a little'.

PUTTING THE HEALTH SERVICE INTO PRACTICE

◆ Hospitals were organised into regional groups and ran by a Regional Board appointed by Bevan. Each hospital had its own management committee.
◆ GPs were watched over by area Executive Councils. They were allowed to keep some of their independence, only part of their pay came from direct salary but most of it depended on the number of patients they had.

◆ Local authorities kept on their Medical Officers who looked after services like vaccination and child care, and also care for the elderly.

BENEFITS TO THE PEOPLE

People now had access to basic health services free of charge:

SOURCE 21.3

... the NHS represented 'the jewel in the crown' of Britain's welfare state.
R Klein in D Gladstone, *The Twentieth Century Welfare State*.

SOURCE 21.4

NHS nursing care.

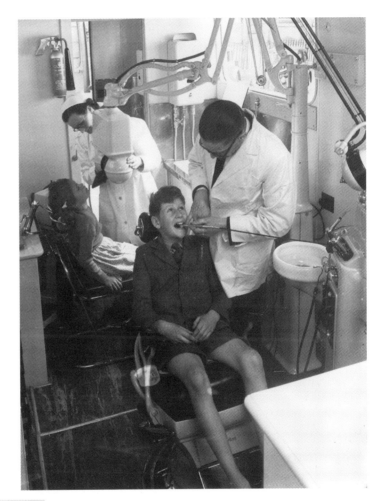

SOURCE 21.5

Dental treatment under the NHS.

PROBLEMS WITH THE NATIONAL HEALTH SERVICE

The Government had hoped that, at first, there would be a high demand for services. But they had expected that as people's needs were met, the costs would quickly drop. However, demand far outstripped Government estimates. The cost of prescriptions alone more than doubled in the months after July 1948. The same pattern was repeated in other services such as the dentists and opticians.

For the cash-strapped Labour Government, the funding of the NHS soon became a real problem. National Insurance health contributions only paid for about 10% of the service's costs, the rest was met out of taxation. Aneurin Bevan was opposed to prescription charges but in 1951 they had to be introduced. Bevan resigned in protest. Source 21.4 below shows the huge increase in welfare spending between 1949 and 1959.

SOURCE 21.4

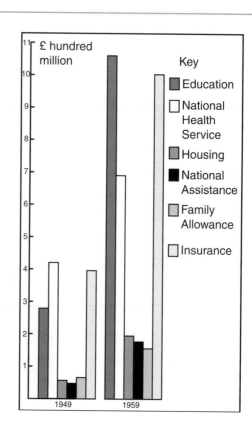

Chapter summary

In this chapter you will have learnt about:

◆ Aneurin Bevan.
◆ The struggle to win over the doctors to the National Health Service.
◆ How Bevan won over the doctors.
◆ How the NHS was organised.
◆ Problems with paying for the NHS.

QUESTION PRACTICE

Intermediate 1

Source A

It is available to the whole population freely ... It is intended that there shall be no limitation on the kind of assistance given, the general practitioner service, the specialist, the hospitals, eye treatment, spectacles, dental treatment, hearing facilities ...
Speech by Bevan about the aims of the NHS

1 What range of services was the NHS going to give to the British people? *Outcome 1*

2 How useful is Source A for the study of the setting up of the NHS? *Outcome 3*

Intermediate 2

DOTHEBOYS HALL
"It still tastes awful."

1 How useful is the cartoon about opposition to the NHS? *Outcome 3*

Source B

A comprehensive health and rehabilitation service was to be made available to all citizens. The local authority health and welfare services included vaccination and immunisation, maternity and child care, domestic help, health visiting, home nursing and ambulances.

2 Describe the benefits of the NHS to the people of Britain. *Outcome 1*

22

THE LABOUR REFORMS: HOUSING AND CHILDREN

In this chapter you will find out about:
- The housing shortage
- 1946 New Towns Act
- 1947 Town and County Planning Act
- 1948 Children Act

HOW DID THE LABOUR GOVERNMENT COPE WITH THE HOUSING SHORTAGE?

The government faced two problems:

1 Many homes had been destroyed during the war.
2 There was a lot of slum housing that still existed from before the war.

The following sources show the scale of the problem faced by the Labour Government:

SOURCE 22.1

Picture of slum housing.

SOURCE 22.2

The generally accepted estimate of 3,000,000 to 4,000,000 houses is a broad indication of the probable housing need during the first 10–12 years of the peace. Aneurin Bevan

Responsibility for housing was given to the Ministry of Health:
- The priority was to house the homeless. So the Ministry continued

the war-time policy of putting up 'pre-fabricated' homes. 'Prefabs' as they were known, were ready-made factory built houses that could be quickly slotted together. They were supposed to be temporary houses but some are still in use today!

◆ Bevan restricted private house building so that building supplies and labour could be used for council housing.

◆ Bevan also tried to improve long-term planning for housing: The 1946 New Towns Act tried to solve the problem of overcrowding in the cities by planning new communities. Twelve new towns were planned. The 1947 Town and Country Planning Act gave councils more planning powers and the ability to buy property in areas they wanted to re-develop.

◆ 1949 Housing Act. Local Authorities were allowed to buy homes for improvement or conversion. 75% of the costs were available from the Government. Private home-owners could get 50% home improvement grants.

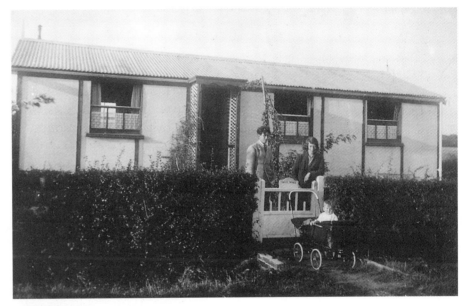

SOURCE 22.3

A prefabricated home.

HOW WELL DID LABOUR MEET THE HOUSING NEED?

◆ The Labour Government made progress with the housing problem in some parts of the country but by 1951 there was still a huge housing shortage in Britain. But on the positive side, the 1946 and 1947 Town and Planning Acts set the basis for town planning for the rest of the century.

◆ Bevan did try to make sure that ordinary workers had good quality homes but demand was so great that the quantity rather than the quality of homes built became the priority.

SOURCE 22.4

Post-war housing in Glasgow.

SOURCE 22.5

From J Hess, *The Social Policy of the Atlee Government.*
The Atlee Government ... did not fulfil its promise to create a Ministry of Housing and Planning ... responsibility for housing remained with the Ministry of Health.

SOURCE 22.6

From J Hess, *The Emergence of the Welfare State in Britain and Germany.*
... Bevan's record as regards house-building was poorer than that of his Conservative successor after 1951 ... but it must not be forgotten that he had to face grave financial and material shortages ... in the circumstances Labour's achievement was rather better than is normally painted.

HOW DID THE LABOUR GOVERNMENT HELP CHILDREN?

EDUCATION

By 1947, the Butler Education Act had been put into practice. The Government also planned a big expansion in further education. The number of student places was increased and a grants system was set up to help children from poorer backgrounds.

CHILD CARE SERVICES

The 1948 Children Act tried to give a better service for children who needed state help and protection. Local councils now had to appoint Children's Officers to ensure decent care for children under the authorities' supervision.

SOURCE 22.7

School milk and meals were provided from 1947.

Chapter summary

In this chapter you will have found out:

◆ How the Labour Government tried to deal with the housing shortage.

◆ How the Labour Government tried to help children.

QUESTION PRACTICE

Intermediate 1

Source A is from G D Simon, *Rebuilding Britain – A 20 Year Plan*.

1. Houses destroyed by bombing.
2. Houses needed to reduce overcrowding.
3. Houses to meet future increase in the number of families.
4. A reserve of empties for flexibility.
5. Additional houses in certain areas to meet any redistribution of the population.
6. Houses needed for slum clearance.

1 Describe the housing problems faced by the Labour Government after 1945. *Outcome 1*

Intermediate 2

Source B Derek Fraser

... most people ... were acutely disappointed in housing ... Labour had promised a massive programme of home building ... but the construction industry was badly hit by a shortage of materials ... though the government's record of house building was better than achieved after the First World War, it did not reach pre-war levels ... local authority building schemes were limited.

1 Explain why people were disappointed in the Government's efforts to solve the housing problem. *Outcome 2*

2 Study Source 22.1. How useful is it in telling you about housing conditions in Scotland after the Second World War? *Outcome 3*

HOW SUCCESSFUL WERE THE LABOUR REFORMS?

THE SUCCESS OF THE WELFARE REFORMS

We will use the 'five giants' of poverty from the Beveridge Report to help us judge the success of Labour's Welfare Reforms:

WANT

Successes:
◆ The National Insurance, Industrial Injuries and National Assistance Acts meant everyone would be given help 'from the cradle to the grave'.

Problems:
◆ The schemes needed a lot of people to administer them.
◆ Not everyone was covered by the National Insurance Act – only those with a certain level of contributions. This meant the 'safety net' did not cover everyone.

DISEASE

Successes:
◆ National Health Service Act 1946. This gave free medical, dental and eye services to all.
◆ The NHS was a huge improvement in the lives of ordinary people.

Problems:
◆ Many of the hospitals were old and not suitable for modern health care.
◆ Financial pressures on the Government meant that most old hospitals were not replaced. The building of new hospitals did not really begin until the 1960s.
◆ The Health Service was a victim of its own success. So many people used the Health Service that it became too expensive for the Government to fund out of taxes alone. Prescription charges were introduced in 1951.

SQUALOR (HOUSING)

Successes:
- It was a main aim of the Labour Government. Bevan, the minister in charge, made sure that prices for building goods and labour were not allowed to become too expensive. This encouraged more building.
- New Towns Act, 1946; twelve new towns planned. 1949 Housing Act; help given to councils and private home-owners for home improvements.
- Between 1948–1951, around 200,000 homes a year were built.
- The number of houses built does not compare with the amount built in the 1930s or 1950s, but the Labour Government made real progress at a time when it was short of materials, workers and money.

Problems:
- Many of the houses built were temporary buildings – prefabs.
- Many families, especially in London, were forced to squat illegally.
- The Government even had to make use of aerodromes which had housed servicemen.
- There was not enough housing to cope with the demobilisation of nearly five million servicemen and women.

IGNORANCE

Successes:
- The Butler Education Act 1944. It was a radical advance in education. It raised the school leaving age. A proper definition of the different stages of education.
- Appropriate education provided for every school pupil.
- Ambitious school building programme.

Problems:
- In practice, the Education Act was not fair. Few working-class children had the chance to go to an academic school. The type of school you went to tended to affect your later opportunities for jobs.
- No attempt to solve differences in educational provision across the country.
- The school building programme concentrated on primary schools to cope with the 'baby boom'. Only 250 secondary schools had been built by the 1950s.

IDLENESS (JOBS)

Successes:
- Government actively promoted a policy of full employment to help support the Welfare State.

◆ Nationalisation of key industries to help full employment.
◆ There was almost full employment after the war despite the post-war economic depression and shortages of goods and materials.
◆ Unemployment was around 2.5%.

Problems:
◆ The British economy and jobs depended heavily on the loans and aid from America.
◆ Women found themselves out of jobs when demobbed servicemen came home. Many women were happy to become housewives again but some found themselves excluded from jobs that they would have liked to continue doing.

HISTORIANS' OPINIONS

Historians have disagreed about how successful the Labour Welfare Reforms were:
In favour of the Labour Reforms:

SOURCE 23.1

From PJ Madgewick et al, *British Political History*.
Poverty was not abolished, but there is no doubt that the number of people seriously lacking in food, clothing, shelter and warmth was substantially reduced compared with the 1930s (or indeed any other period).

SOURCE 23.2

From D Coates, *The Labour Party and the Struggle for Socialism*.
It created a system of universally available social insurance, which provided minimum incomes and pensions to those subject to ill-health, industrial accidents, disablement, infirmity and old age.

Against the Labour Reforms:
One historian, Corelli Barnett, believes that the Welfare State only succeeded in crushing individual responsibility and creating dependency on the state:

SOURCE 23.3

... the subliterate, unskilled, unhealthy and institutionalised proletariat hanging on the nipple of state maternalism.

Barnett also believes that Bevan and the Labour Government failed to do proper calculations about how much the NHS and other services would cost:

SOURCE 23.4

Why then did Bevan, abetted by his advisers, so completely fail to carry out an operational analysis of the likely scales and types of demands, coupled with a calculation of the logistical resources needed? ... Could it be that, given Britain's precarious finances, even a Cabinet dedicated to the New Jerusalem might have baulked if presented with a realistic estimate of the cost of the NHS?

Chapter summary

In this chapter you will have learned:

◆ The Labour Government had mixed success in dealing with the 'five giants' of poverty.

◆ Historians have criticised and praised the achievements of the Labour Government.

◆ Despite problems with the reforms, the Labour Government, 1945–51 are to be praised for their attempt to provide universal care 'from the cradle to the grave'.

Historians seem to disagree because they judge the reforms of the Labour Government, 1945–51 by different standards. One historian believes that Labour were a success because they were trying something new:

SOURCE 23.5

From P Thane, *The Foundations of the Welfare State.*
The social reforms of the Labour Government were a profound improvement on what had gone before, but they were only a first step ... It was the universality of provision of health care, social security and education ... which constituted the claim of the post-war Labour Governments to have established ... a new approach to the use of the power of the state consciously in the interests of social justice for the mass of the population, a 'welfare state'.

QUESTION PRACTICE

Summary and Review Exercise

1 Copy out the table. Use the heading 'Labour's Welfare Achievements, 1945–1951'. Under the column 'Reform and Progress Made', note down the reforms made by the Labour Government for each of the policies mentioned. Two of the boxes have been filled in for you.

2 This will be an extended response question. Use the subheadings on Beveridge's five giants of poverty in this chapter, to help you structure your answer. Remember to add your own introduction and conclusion. The question is:

How far did Labour's Welfare Reforms go to dealing with the Five Giants of poverty?

Policy	Reform and Progress Made
Full employment	Unemployment rarely rose above 2% of the workforce.
Nationalisation	
National Health Service	
Housing	
Education	School leaving age raised to 15.
Planning	

Building of Welfare State benefits:
    Unemployment
    Sickness
    Injury Compensation
    National Assistance	

CONCLUSION

By 1951, the reforms that made up the Welfare State had been put into practice. The Labour Party deserves much of the credit for the Welfare State: it was its determination that drove through the reforms despite political opposition, a poor economy and international problems. But the Labour Government also built on the policies of the Liberals and Conservatives. They too had been greatly concerned with improving the lives of people in need through health, housing and education.

The achievement of the Labour Government and the Welfare State by 1951 was clear: for the majority of people, life had greatly improved. In 1950, Seebohm Rowntree did a third study of York. He found that old people still struggled, but that poor pay, overcrowding, unemployment and poverty were not as serious as they once were. Even for the elderly, their lives were more dignified and comfortable than ever before.

Government power and control over people's lives greatly increased in the period, 1890–1951. But so did expectations of a Government's responsibility to help its citizens. In particular, the Second World War was a real turning point in changing people's attitudes towards a Government's social responsibility. The Beveridge Report rightly deserves the credit for focusing public attention on how best to tackle the problems of poverty.

Ever since the creation of the Welfare State people have continued to argue about how help should be given to those in need, how best to cope with issues like the following:

◆ Should flat rate benefits, like the Family Allowance, be given to everyone, even if they don't need it?
◆ Have state benefits made people too dependent on government help?
◆ How do you decide when a person is 'in need'?
◆ Should the definition of poverty change as standards of living rise?
◆ How do you decide the right levels of benefit – that prevent poverty but still give an incentive to work?
◆ Should the Welfare State be more selective in whom it helps?

We may never find ideal answers to these questions. But the reforms of 1890–1951 have left a permanent mark on our society. We take it for granted that help should be given to those in need and that the Government should give state benefits. Despite attacks on the Welfare System in recent years, we remain a society giving help 'from the cradle to the grave'.

TEST AND EXAM ADVICE

There are three basic types of question. They are listed below together with a description of what you must do for each type of question. What you must achieve for each type of question is called an 'outcome'. *Parts in italics are only needed for Intermediate 2.* The length of answer will depend on the number of marks. Try to include at least one developed point for each mark.

Outcome 1
Description questions which ask you to show your knowledge and understanding of historical developments, events and issues.

a) you must use recalled knowledge which is relevant to the question; at Intermediate 1 you must also use relevant information from the source(s).
b) your knowledge from recall (and the source(s) at Intermediate 1) must show accurate understanding of the topic and its themes and issues.

Outcome 2
Explanation questions which ask you to explain historical developments and events. You usually have to explain the reasons for, or the results of something.

a) Int. 1 and 2 – your explanation must be supported by accurate and relevant information from recall and the source(s).
b) *Int. 2 only – your answer for the 8-mark short essay question must have an introduction and a conclusion (see page 103)*

Outcome 3
Source evaluation questions which ask you to evaluate historical sources with reference to their context (what was happening at the time). These usually ask you how useful, reliable or accurate a source is.

a) Int. 1 – your evaluation must take into account the origin or purpose of the source (Who wrote it? When was it written? Why was it written? etc.).
   Int. 2 – you must also take into account the context of the source(s) (relevant information about what was happening at the time).
b) Int. 1 – your evaluation must show you understand what is in the source.

*Int. 2 — your evaluation must take into account the content of
the source. You can also point out what the source fails to
mention.*

c) *Int. 2 only – you must be able to make an accurate comparison
between two sources.*

HOW TO WRITE YOUR 8-MARK ESSAY

One of the questions in internal tests and the final exam at
Intermediate 2 is the 8-mark essay question.

It is an explanation type of question for which you usually have
to explain the reasons for or result of something.

Remember that your essay
◆ must have an introduction
◆ must have a middle section with paragraphs for each of your
  main points
◆ must have a separate conclusion.

Making a plan
It often helps to jot down a list of about five main points you want
to deal with before you start your essay. You can add to the list if
more points occur to you.

Introduction: This is worth 1 or 2 marks
It should deal with the question. It might only be a sentence or two.
You could start with a sentence like this: *'There were many reasons
why ... (such and such happened). These reasons were ...'*

Middle section: This is worth 5 marks
If you have five main points you should have five paragraphs in the
middle section of your essay. Each paragraph should start with a
sentence, which sets out what the paragraph will be about. You
should then explain what your main point means or how it is
connected to the question. You should then go on to use accurate
and relevant facts to explain what you mean and show off what you
know.

Conclusion: This is worth 1 or 2 marks
It should be a paragraph of a few sentences and should sum up your
answer. It could be something like: *'In conclusion, there were lots of
reasons why (such and such happened). These reasons included ...
(sum up your main points).'*
In your conclusion you should:
◆ Sum up the points you have explained earlier in the answer. You
  could also say which points you think were the most important
  and give reasons.
◆ Make your mind up and answer the question that you were
  asked.
Use this pattern for all your 8-mark essays. You can also use it to

help you with your extended response. Remember you only have to do one 8-mark essay in the exam. Use the advice on this page to get it right.

The following example shows how an 8-mark essay can be organised. The question is:

Why did the Liberals pass so many social reforms, 1906–1914?

Introduction

You could start with a sentence like this:
There are several reasons why the Liberals passed so many social reforms between 1906 and 1914. These reasons were . . .

Then briefly summarise them.

Middle section

Here you need a paragraph for each of the reasons mentioned in your introduction. Each paragraph could start with a main sentence that says what the paragraph will be about.

Your first paragraph could start like this:
The first reason why the Liberals passed social reforms was because evidence from social investigators like Booth and Rowntree meant that something had to be done.

Use your knowledge to explain this more fully. Then go on to the next reason. You might choose, for example, to deal with the Boer War next. Take each reason in turn in this way.

Conclusion

Your conclusion should sum up your answer. It could be something like this:

There were many causes of the Liberal social reforms. By 1906 the evidence for the amount of poverty provided by Booth and Rowntree shocked people at the time. Many Liberals like Lloyd George and Winston Churchill had genuine concern for the poor and wanted to do something to help them. There were also worries about the British Empire. Recruits for the Boer War were often rejected because they were unfit. An unfit army would not be able to defend the Empire. It also meant the workforce was weak, which would lead to economic decline. Finally, the electorate was demanding change. The new Labour Party was growing in size and the Liberals were worried about losing working-class voters. This made them willing to pass social reforms.

A conclusion like this brings together the main points in a very clear way and directly answers the question. Now try to write a full answer to the question above.

EXTENDED RESPONSE ADVICE

Intermediate 2 candidates must also produce a longer prepared essay as part of the external course assessment – usually round about February/March.

This is called the Extended Response and is worth one quarter of the final marks. It is similar to the 8-mark short essay (see page 103). The main differences are:

◆ It will be much longer than an 8-mark short essay. You will have an hour to write it. It could be up to 1,000 words long (four or five sides of A4).

◆ You choose your own question relating to one of the three units making up your course. Your teacher can advise you on this.

◆ You research and prepare your answer by reading and taking notes from a variety of sources. Your teacher can help you with sources.

◆ You prepare a plan of 150 words with sub-headings, which you can take into the final writing-up session. Your teacher can check your plan for you.

◆ A teacher will supervise the final one-hour writing-up session under exam conditions, but cannot help you in any way. Your plan and response are then sent to the SQA for marking.

CHOOSING A QUESTION

◆ Pick a topic that interests you and that you feel you can do well in.

◆ Discuss the exact wording of the question with your teacher.

◆ Choose a question that requires you to explain and assess what happened rather than simply describing events.

◆ Avoid questions which cover too much or which are too vague or too narrow.

◆ You should be able to divide it up into about five sub-headings.

◆ Some possible questions for this unit are given on the next page.

READING AND NOTE-TAKING

Talk to your teacher about sources.

As you read, jot down notes for your different sub-headings (using separate sheets for each sub-heading or by indicating in the margin which sub-heading each note is about). Use key words and avoid copying whole sentences and paragraphs – try to use one or two good short 'quotes'.

PREPARING YOUR PLAN

Use your notes to prepare your 150-word plan. This should consist of sub-headings and key points to remind you of what you want to include. You could also draw a spider diagram like the one on the next page to help you.

If you want, you can write a practice draft of your full response, but you cannot take it into the final write-up session with you. You are only allowed to take in your plan of not more than 150 words.

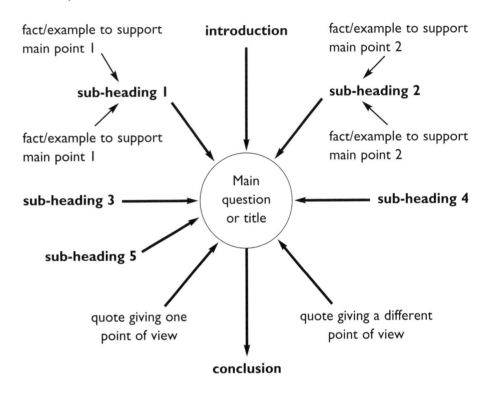

THE WRITE-UP SESSION

- Your plan will enable you to work your way steadily through your response.
- You have one hour to do this, allowing about ten minutes for each sub-heading and leaving time for your conclusion.
- Try to concentrate on explanation and analysis rather than just description and narrative.
- If you are running out of time, make quick notes about any remaining sub-headings and go straight to your conclusion.

POSSIBLE EXTENDED RESPONSE QUESTIONS

- Why were people in Britain becoming concerned about poverty by 1900?
- How important were the social investigations of Booth and Rowntree in changing attitudes towards poverty?
- What were the main reasons for the Liberal Reform programme of 1906–14?
- How important were Lloyd George and Winston Churchill to the Liberal Reforms of 1906–14?
- Why is the National Insurance Act of 1911 so important?

♦ In what ways did the Liberal Reforms help poor people?
♦ How successful were the Liberal Reforms in tackling problems of poverty?
♦ For what reasons had attitudes to Welfare changed by 1945?
♦ How important was the Second World War to the setting up of the Welfare State?
♦ Why was the Beveridge Report so important for the Welfare State?
♦ What problems did the Labour Government of 1945–51 face when setting up the Welfare State?
♦ Why did Bevan have so many problems creating the NHS?
♦ Is it true to say that the Labour Government (1945–51) deserves all the credit for setting up the Welfare State?
♦ Were the Labour Reforms successful?
♦ How well did the Labour Government tackle the 'five giants' of poverty?

A NOTE ON SOURCES AND SUPPORT MATERIAL

The difficulty with many of the Sources for this topic is that they are written in a style that is hard to understand.

SUPPORT

The HSDU pack on *Intermediate 1 & 2* on *From the Cradle to the Grave?* Social Welfare in Britain 1890s–1951, provides useful sources and tasks for the major reforms.

PRIMARY SOURCES

Useful collections of documents can be found in the following:

Into Unknown England 1866–1913, edited by Peter Keating (A Fontana original).
(Useful for the studies of poverty. However, the sources are very long.)

Documents from Edwardian England by Donald Read (George G. Harrap & Co. Ltd, 1973).
(Useful for documents concerning poverty and Liberal Reforms.)

Social Policy, 1830–1914: Individualism, collectivism and the origins of the Welfare State, edited by Eric J. Evans (Routledge and Kegan Paul Ltd, 1978).
(Useful for documents with good introductions to the chapters.)

Social Welfare in Britain, 1885–1985, edited by Rex Pope, Alan Pratt and Bernard Hoyle (printed by Croom Helm Ltd, 1986).
(Useful but the sources are quite difficult in terms of length.)

The Evolution of the British Welfare State by Derek Fraser (Macmillan, 1974) has useful documents at the back of the book, as does *The Shaping of the Welfare State* by R.C. Birch (Longman, 1974).
(Useful but the sources are quite difficult in terms of length.)

Signs of the Times: Sources in Modern History: British Political History, 1900–51 by David Adelman (Hodder & Stoughton, 1991).
(Extremely useful for photographs, primary evidence and historians' opinions.)

Scotland's War by Seona Robertson and Les Wilson (Mainstream Publishing, 1995).
(Excellent for the ordinary Scottish person's perspective on the impact of the war. Good quotes and photographs.)

SECONDARY SOURCES

Many secondary sources are serious academic books. The best of those consulted include:

Modern Britain: A Social History; 1750–1985, by Edward Royale (Edward Arnold, 1987).
(Reasonably clear and readable survey.)

The British Welfare State 1900–1950 by Sydney Wood (Cambridge University Press, 1982).
(Clear survey with useful summaries of reforms.)

The Origins of the Liberal Welfare Reforms 1906–14 by J. R. Hay (Macmillan, 1975).
(Difficult but thorough text.)

The Evolution of the British Welfare State by Derek Fraser (Macmillan, 1971).
(An excellent survey but difficult.)

The Foundations of the Welfare State by Pat Thane (Longman, 1982).
(Good for teachers rather than students.)

The Shaping of the Welfare State by R.C. Birch (Longman, 1974).
(Good for research, quite an academic style.)

The Five Giants, a Biography of the Welfare state by N. Timmins (Harper Collins, 1995).
(A large book but good on historians' opinions and for primary sources.)

The Twentieth Century Welfare State by David Gladstone (Macmillan 1999).
(An academic book but good on historians' opinions.)

OTHER SOURCES:

Memory Lane: A photographic Album of Daily Life In Britain, 1930–1953 by James Cameron (J.M. Dent and Sons 1980).

CD Rom: Scottish People 1840–1940, A Social and Economic History.

Visual Support

BBC Television has also provided support with two Intermediate History programmes on *The Liberal Reforms* and *The Welfare State*. These are excellent and provide good key questions and summaries.

Useful web addresses
For research on subjects from Booth to Churchill:
http://www.lib.gcal.ac.uk/heatherbank/
http://www.museum.scotland.net/
http://www.mitchelllibrary.org/vm/searches/subjects.html
http://www.churchill.nls.ac.uk/
http://booth.lse.ac.uk/

GLOSSARY

abetted	helped
acknowledge	to recognise or agree with something
administer	to organise
baulked	refused or resisted
comprehensive	can mean to include everything or refer to schools where children of all abilities go to the one school
compulsory	when something has to be done
conscription	the calling up of men and women to join the armed services during wartime
credibility	the extent to which someone or something is believable
development	change
economic depression	a period of time when the country's industries find it hard to find buyers for their products, often leading to unemployment
economy	the jobs and money provided by industry
ferocious	fierce
Government	the political party elected by the people at general elections to run the country
insurance	payments made by people, or organisations, into a fund of money. In times of unemployment or ill health, money could be taken out of this fund if enough contributions had been made
legislation	another word for laws or reforms
magnitude	large size
national efficiency	the belief that Britain was becoming less powerful as a result of poverty. This had affected her economic power and her military power
obligation	a task or responsibility that has to be done
pauperism	where people were extremely poor and without the ability to earn any money
Poor Law	the law which set out how the poor should be treated in the 19th century
poverty	when people find themselves unable to eat, clothe and house themselves properly
precarious	unsafe or insecure
prescription charges	charge made by the Government to help the cost of medicine ordered by the doctor
priority	main need or aim
reforms	changes in law approved by Parliament
rehabilitation	to make well again
reverence	respect
salary	yearly wage paid by an employer
slums	housing that is unfit for people to live in or is in a very poor state of repair

social investigator	term given to people who studied poverty. Booth and Rowntree are very good examples of this sort of person
social security	the help given by the Government to make sure that even the poorest income does not fall below a certain level
society	the British people. Usually used when talking about national action or community responsibility
state	another word for government
universality	applied to everyone
Welfare State	this term can refer to an ideal of help that society should provide and the state benefits provided by the Government

Index